Praise for *The Green Parent*

"As thoughtful stewards of the little people we care for and of the planet we inhabit, we want to tread lightly. In *The Green Parent*, author Jenn Savedge guides us through how to live "green" and pass that love and respect for the earth on to our children—whether it's working with our kids' school to ensure anti-idling, planning an eco-family vacation or finding an earth-friendly (and scalp-friendly!) way of dealing with head lice. Savedge writes with an infectious optimism that motivates us to change our ways…and change the world in the process."

–Leslie Garrett, journalist and author of *The Virtuous Consumer*,
mother of three

"*The Green Parent* is an excellent guide for parents! Savedge provides an encyclopedic approach to a range of issues from energy efficiency to saving money. For people who don't have time to research environmental issues, this book boils them down to their key components, then offers easy solutions that any parent can manage. The simple format and step-by-step suggestions make this a nifty resource to read cover-to-cover, and then use as a reference guide whenever you need just the right answer. Savedge includes fun ideas like a "Light Patrol" badge to get kids involved in saving energy, as well as ideas for throwing a "green" party. She covers very practical ideas too, like how to get rid of head lice in an environmentally friendly way. I've dog-eared many pages in this book and always keep it close at hand."

–Kathleen Ridihalgh, www.greatgreentips.net, mother of one

"How many times have parents told children to mind their manners? In *The Green Parent* the roles are reversed. This thoughtful must-have book for parents reminds us of the old Native American saying: We do not inherit the Earth from our Ancestors; we borrow it from our Children. Parents, mind your environmental manners!"

–Doug Farr, author of *Sustainable Urbanism: Urban Design with Nature*

"*The Green Parent* is a great resource for parents looking to incorporate Earth-friendliness into their lives. It offers lots of creative, sensible and easy-to-do ideas that all families—whether they're eco-experts or green at being green—can weave into the fabric of their daily lives."

–Corey Colwell-Lipson & Lynn Colwell, authors of *Celebrate Green*,
www.thegreenyear.com

"The decisions parents make regarding how they raise their children can have a significant impact on the environment. This book is a great resource to guide parents to more environmentally friendly choices."

—Sadhu Johnston, Chief Environmental Officer, City of Chicago, father of one

"*The Green Parent* is a fabulous read for parents who are trying to improve the health of their children, household, communities and planet! The organization of material makes it a snap to find what you are looking for and the interviews with real parents doing the real work of "going green" helps the reader see the reality behind what is too easily brushed off as utopian thinking. It is wonderful that Ms. Savedge gives ideas to get the *kids themselves* involved (a parenting book is about guiding the next generation, after all) and her guide to labels, both real and misleading, will help parents where the rubber meets the road...while shopping. Each chapter ends with a list of additional resources, so you are all set to get as green as you want!"

—Lee Welles, author of the *Gaia Girls Book Series*

"A great resource for updated details on green living—especially useful for parents who no longer have the time to stay in the loop on best practices."

—Sara Prout, Development Officer, Bainbridge Graduate Institute, mother of three

"It is important to raise our children in a way that is good for their health and good for the environment. In addition, the way we live our lives will serve as a model for how our children will live. *The Green Parent* is an excellent resource for parents that is both subtle and compelling. It doesn't hit you over the head with guilt, but instead lifts you up with the possibilities of how to live your lives in an environmentally reasonable way."

—Suzanne Malec-McKenna, Commissioner of Environment, City of Chicago, mother of one.

"*The Green Parent* offers clear and practical ways for families to help the environment. The book includes great facts, analysis, tips, and activities for reducing your consumption and making the most of what you do consume. Parents who start off by following even a few of Jenn Savedge's tips will not only help save the planet for our children, but will have a more joyous family life for the effort."

—Raj Mankad and Miah Arnold, authors of the Green Parenting blog, http://grizzlybird.net/greenparenting/

kedzie press

Million Tree-A-Thon

You Buy the Books · We Plant the Trees

In collaboration with Eco-Libris, Kedzie Press has embarked on the Kedzie Million Tree-A-Thon, with the goal of planting one million trees by December 2009. As a result of purchasing this book, Kedzie Press will pay to have one tree planted. Thank you for joining the race!

For more information, visit www.kedziepress.com. For details on when and how the trees will be planted, please visit our friends at Eco-Libris at www.ecolibris.net.

This book is printed on Rolland Enviro100. This paper is 100% recycled, containing 100% post consumer waste fiber, Processed Chlorine Free, EcoLogo, FSC Recycled certified and manufactured using biogas.

The author has chosen to donate a portion of her royalties from this title to the DJ Johnson Memorial Fund at the Victim's Resource Center (www.vrcnepa.org). Kedzie Press will match all funds donated.

The Green Parent

A Kid-Friendly Guide
to Earth-Friendly Living

The Green Parent

A Kid-Friendly Guide to Earth-Friendly Living

by Jenn Savedge

kedziepress
Seattle

Published by Kedzie Press LLC
535 Pontius Avenue N., Suite 126
Seattle, WA 98109
www.kedziepress.com

This book is printed with soy-based inks on Roland Enviro 100. The paper consists of 100% recycled fiber content made from 100% post-consumer waste, and is Processed Chlorine Free.

The publisher would like to acknowledge the efforts of Lori Rennie and Transcontinental Printing for their continued dedication to working towards an environmentally feasible publishing future.

In collaboration with Eco-Libris, one tree will be planted within one year of the sale of this copy. For more information on Eco-Libris, visit their website at www.ecolibris.net.

Cover and interior design by Patricia Rasch
"Green Parent" logo design by Nicoletta Barolini
Author photo by: Eileen Carlock

Library of Congress Cataloging-in-Publication Data

Savedge, Jenn, 1972-
The green parent : a kid-friendly guide to Earth-friendly living / by Jenn Savedge.
p. cm.
ISBN 978-1-934087-22-0 (alk. paper)
1. Environmental responsibility. 2. Sustainable living. 3. Green movement. 4. Education--Parent participation. I. Title.
GE195.7.S28 2008
333.72--dc22
2007047403

10 9 8 7 6 5 4 3 2 1

Printed in Canada

Acknowledgements

I am a lucky woman. I have a great family that I love (and that loves me back) and I have a job that entails researching and writing about the two issues that are most dear to my heart, my children and the environment. Like any mom, I have a vast network of friends and family to thank for all of this luck.

First and foremost, I want to thank my girls, for their patience, understanding, and overwhelming support of this project. I could not be a Green Parent without them! I also owe an enormous debt of gratitude to my family: to my husband for keeping me sane (!) and putting up with my eco-nagging; to my mom for her unwavering encouragement and for listening to all of my eco-babble; and to my mom and dad-in-law for their support and tireless grandparent energy.

I am exceedingly grateful to my editor, Jessica Sanchez, who gave me the opportunity to turn an idea into a book and then guided, encouraged, and motivated me through every phase of the project. I also want to thank Megan Williams, who gave of her precious kid-free time to help me nurture *The Green Parent* from a scattered assortment of notes into a full-fledged book. And thank you as well to her family for their suggestions and ideas.

Thank you to all of the folks whose technical expertise polished this book and made it shine: Patricia Rasch, Angela Cardoz, Rose Sell, Nicoletta Barolini, and Dawn Hickerson. Thanks to Eileen Carlock for her creative magic in turning a cranky family into a "Happy Green Family" (at least in pictures). And a special thanks to Brenda Long and all of the staff at 58 West Café for giving me the nutritional and technical sustenance I needed to write.

I also want to thank Josh Dorfman who parlayed his knowledge as a "Lazy Environmentalist" into knowledge that a "Harried, Overextended, Green Parent" could use. And thank you to all of the Green Parents who generously gave of their time and motivated me to be a deeper shade of green, namely, Colin Beaven (No Impact Man), Jason Brown (*Organics to Go*), Corey Colwell-Lipson (*Green Halloween*), Alan Durning (*The Year of Living Car-lessly*), Leslie Garrett (The Virtuous Consumer), Lori Helman(*Mommas Baby*), Michael Lackman (Lotus Organics), Bill McKibben (*The End of Nature*), Kathleen Ridihalgh (*Great Green Tips*), David Steinman (*The Safe Shopper's Bible*) and Timberly Whitfield (*New Morning*).

My village also included the help of a number of people whose support makes me a better mom and a better person, and therefore a better writer, specifically, James Krackow, Marisa Ramos, Nancy Savedge, Theresa Dispenzirie, Ellen Creveling, Alexa Bonomo, Deanna Pavlik, Brooke Downing, Heather Davis, Sheryl Hunsberger, Missy Forder, Liz Lewis, Donna Gessner, and all of the ladies of the Luray Mom's Club.

For Emily and Erin

Table of Contents

The Green Parent's Top 10

1. Talk To Your Kids About The Environment
(Ch. 1-17)

2. Leave Your Car Behind (Ch. 8)

3. Reuse And Then Recycle (Ch. 1-19)

4. B.Y.O.B. (Bag/Bottle) (Ch. 2, 3, 9, 10, 12)

5. Install CFLs (Ch. 1)

6. Go Paperless (Ch. 3)

7. Make A Waste-Free Lunch (Ch. 3)

8. Buy Organic (Ch. 12-17)

9. Go Light On Your Lawncare (Ch. 5)

10. Keep Learning (Ch. 18)

Why Go Green?

According to the U.S. Environmental Protection Agency, Americans throw out enough wood and paper each year to supply a year's worth of heat to a billion homes and enough aluminum to quadruple the size of our airline fleet. Americans use roughly 70 million pounds of pesticides (ten times the amount used on farms) to keep their lawns green. And the average American family's energy use generates over 11,200 pounds of air pollutants each year.

No parent wants to raise their child in a world full of toxins. Yet we are often too overwhelmed by the magnitude of environmental concerns and what we perceive as the necessary steps that must be undertaken by communities, industries, and the government to make a difference. Environmental issues such as global warming, hazardous waste, loss of rain forests, endangered species, acid rain, the ozone layer, and heaving landfills feel out of our control. There is just too much trash, too much pollution, too few resources, and too little time to really make a difference, right? WRONG!

As a busy parent, you may not have time to spend hours researching what you could do to protect the environment. Should you buy organic or buy local? Which items are the most important to recycle? How can you get the most green for your green? Let's face it, in the modern household, time is as precious a commodity as any other. But the fact of the matter is, whether you are raising an infant or a teenager, the decisions you make each day affect the environment. And even small changes can make a big difference.

For instance, recycling just one soda can saves enough energy to run a 100-watt bulb for 20 hours, a computer for three hours, or a TV for two hours. Recycling one ton of paper (the average family uses 1.3 tons each year) would save enough landfill space to hold 64 tall kitchen garbage bags and enough energy to heat an average home for six months. And just taking the time to fix the leaky faucets and toilets around your house can save over 4,500 gallons of water each year, conserving resources and reducing pollution.

But just how important is it to protect the environment? As a parent, you are already pulled in several directions at once, trying to balance the financial, nutritional, educational, recreational, and spiritual needs of your family. Do you really need to add one more item to your ever-expanding to-do list? Here are six great reasons to go green:

Going Green Saves Green

The essence of going green is to use less: less electricity, less water, and less stuff. And the good news is that using less actually saves you money. Conserve energy and you'll have a lower electric bill and need less fuel at the pump. Reduce waste and you'll spend less money at the store and have lower trash removal fees. And fix your leaky faucets and you'll not only conserve water, you'll also slash the cost of your annual water bill. Now, who couldn't use a little more green?

A Clean Bill of Health

We rely on the environment for more than aesthetics and commodities. It is literally the air we breathe, the food we eat, and the water we drink. Air pollution, global warming, acid rain, and water pollution deteriorate the environment as well as human health. Protecting the environment means protecting these resources and ensuring that your family has access to clean water, healthy foods, and fresh air.

It's For The Birds

Contrary to popular belief, we are not the only species on the planet. Every bird, mammal, fish, and tree depends upon the environment for its survival. And even if you are not an avid bird-watcher, the survival of one species is linked to the survival of the others. You may not notice when one plant or bird species becomes extinct, but as the number of threatened species on the planet rises, the pressure on the environment builds up, affecting the survival of humans.

So You Can Look Your Kids In The Eye

There is an old Native American adage that says, "We did not inherit the Earth from our parents, we are borrowing it from our children." One of our obligations as parents is to ensure that our children have the same access to nature that we enjoy. When you are old and gray and bouncing your grandkids on your lap, you'll be glad that they are growing up in a clean, healthy environment, and that the actions you took made it that way.

Raising 'Em Right

No matter how hard you try to teach your children to do the right thing, they will inevitably learn from what you do rather than what you say. If you show your children that you care about the environment by making environmentally friendly choices, they will follow your lead. Raising children who understand their connection to the environment is one of the most eco-friendly impacts you can make.

Give The Economy A Boost

You do not have to choose between protecting the environment and supporting the economy. Eco-friendly choices drive a free-market economy. Industries such as farming, fishing, and tourism rely on the health of the environment. Innovative technologies and products that protect the environment create new high-paying jobs. Using the marketplace for eco-friendly products is a win-win solution for consumers and businesses. So by going green, you help to foster a strong economy.

Environmental issues such as waste reduction, global warming, water conservation, and air pollution may seem too overwhelming to tackle alone. But there are many simple things that you can do every day to benefit the environment. Carpool with another family to soccer practice and you'll reduce air pollution, conserve energy, and slow global warming. Recycle your daily newspaper and you'll conserve resources, reduce energy costs, and save on landfill space. The list of possibilities is endless, and as parents, the choices are yours. Every small change you make can make a huge difference for the environment. Are you ready to get started? Let this book be your guide.

Chapter 1:

Save Energy, Save Money, Save The Planet

It takes a lot of energy to raise a child. No kidding, right? It takes an enormous amount of physical energy to keep up with (and stay one step ahead of) your kids. But you also need a lot of energy in the form of fossil fuels (coal, oil, or natural gas) for the electricity required to keep your kids warm, cool, clean, clothed, and fed. The average American family's energy use damages water resources, contributing to global warming, deteriorating human health, triggering acid rain, and damaging habitat for wildlife.

Americans use nearly a million dollars worth of energy every minute, night and day, every day of the year, with the largest portion of the energy bill going towards keeping the home a comfortable temperature. Heating accounts for 66% of your annual energy bill, followed by 22% for air conditioning. Other big energy users are appliances and the hot water heater. Every kilowatt you conserve and every battery you save can significantly trim your monthly energy bill while helping to protect the planet. Here are some easy ideas for reducing energy consumption in your home.

Top 5 Ways To Make An Impact

1. **Control Your Temperature:** Two thirds of your home's energy consumption is used to keep you warm and another big chunk is used to keep you cool. Even a minor adjustment in your thermostat can slash your energy use. During the summer months, bump up the thermostat to 78 degrees and open the windows when there is a fresh breeze. In the winter, set it to around 68 degrees and turn it down even more (try 55 degrees) when you go to sleep or are away for the day.

2. **Pull The Plug:** Even when appliances are off, they are still draining energy in "standby" mode. Use a power strip to turn off televisions, stereos, and computer systems when you are not using them and unplug appliances such as phone chargers, extra refrigerators, and printers until you need them.

3. **Install CFLs:** Consider swapping out regular light bulbs for energy-saving, long-lasting compact fluorescents (CFLs) to save both energy and cash. CFLs cost a few cents more than standard bulbs, but they require about ¼ of the energy to produce the same amount and quality of light, and they last ten times as long (saving you money down the road).

4. **Buy ENERGY STAR Appliances:** There is now an energy-efficient alternative for almost every kind of appliance or light fixture, so you don't need to forgo convenience in order to save energy. Check out the U.S. Department of Energy's ENERGY STAR program (**www.energystar.gov**) to find a list of appliances that use less energy than standard models. Of course, it doesn't make ecological or financial sense to throw good stuff

away. If your toaster is running fine, don't toss it, but look for the star the next time you need to replace it.

5. **Support Renewable Energy:** If your local utility offers you a choice, select renewable energy or purchase green credits to offset your energy use (See **Greensourcing** in this chapter).

Green Tips

HEATING AND AIR CONDITIONING

Adjust Your Drapes

In the summer, keep the drapes closed over sunny windows to reduce heat from the sun. If you live in a warm climate, take advantage of drapes with an insulating lining that will keep the sun's rays from heating your home. In the winter, take advantage of the sun's energy by leaving shades and blinds open on sunny days, and then closing them at night to reduce heat loss.

Close It Off

Cut your energy costs further by making sure the hot (or cold) air stays where you need it. If you have rooms in your house that you rarely go into (i.e. any rooms that aren't "kid-proofed"), keep them sealed off by closing doors and air vents.

Feeling Dirty?

Clean the filters on heating and air conditioning units to keep them operating efficiently. Dirty filters make your air conditioners and hot-air furnaces work harder and use more energy. Cleaning a dirty air conditioner filter can reduce energy use by 5%.

Insulate Yourself

Simple steps like insulating and weather stripping can reduce your energy use by 20%-30%. Caulk and weather-strip around doors and windows to stop air leaks. Door sweeps are an easy cheap solution for drafty doors. Storm windows and doors can reduce heat loss by 30%.

Be sure to install appropriate insulation in your walls and ceiling for the climate in your area to improve your home's energy efficiency. You don't even have to tear down walls to add insulation. Contractors can pump foam insulation into a one-inch hole in your wall, insulating the whole house in just a few hours.

If you want to make sure your house is sealed off, consider hiring an energy rater who can use special equipment to test your house for hidden leaks. In California, contact the California Home Energy Rating Services (www.cheers.org); elsewhere contact Residential Energy Services Network (www.resnet.us) to find a certified energy rater in your area, or check out The Home Energy Saver's online energy auditing tool, http://hes.lbl.gov/hes/.

APPLIANCES

Put Your Fridge On A Diet

Refrigerators suck down energy to keep our food cold. If your fridge is equipped with a power-saving feature, use it. Set your refrigerator temperature at 38 to 42 degrees Fahrenheit; your freezer should be set between 0 and 5 degrees Fahrenheit. Keep an eye on the items in your refrigerator or freezer any time you change the temperature to be sure that nothing spoils prematurely (especially if you have an older unit that may not be as precise on the temperature gauge, or as efficient as a newer model). If you have an extra refrigerator that you're not using, unplug it. Keep your refrigerator full, but don't overfill it. Air needs room to circulate around food. Keep the freezer full as well to maximize efficiency. Check the gaskets around your fridge to make sure they are clean and tight to lock in cold air. Here's the test: Close a dollar bill in the refrigerator door with part of it sticking out. If it is difficult to pull out, the gaskets are sealing properly. If it pulls out easily, it's time to replace them.

Cook Up Some Energy Savings

Use the right size pot for the job (the larger the pot, the more energy it will use when heating it up). Use a pot with a flat bottom that completely covers the burner and put a lid on it to keep heat from escaping (this will also cook your food more quickly). Since your food may heat up quickly when covered, keep a close eye on your pots and pans during cooking. You'd hate to have your pots boil over or your dinner burn! If you have a gas range, lower the flame if it is burning around the side of your pot or pan.

Take a few minutes to clean and maintain your oven and you can greatly improve its energy efficiency. As much as I'd love to tell you otherwise, a dirty oven does not reflect heat as well as a clean one. That means it will have to use more energy to heat up and stay warm. Also, check the seal on your oven door to make sure all of that heat is staying inside. When you are baking, if possible, skip the preheating step. Most recipes don't really need it anyhow. And resist the temptation to peek inside your oven any more than necessary, even opening the door just once can cause the temperature inside to drop considerably.

Green Dishes?

Don't run your dishwasher unless it's full. When you do run it, set it to the shortest setting for all but the dirtiest dishes. Avoid using energy-sucking options such as heat-dry, rinse-hold, and pre-rinse features. If you have time, let your dishes air-dry to reduce your dishwasher's total energy use by 20%.

Ride The Wave

For cooking or reheating small items, microwave foods instead of heating them in the stove or oven. This can reduce energy use by 75%.

Green Washing

Wash your clothes in cold water whenever practical and make sure your machine is set to always rinse in cold. Set your washer to the appropriate water level for the size of your load. When you're in the market for a new machine, consider a front loading washer that cuts hot water use by 60%-70%.

Clean the lint filter in your dryer after each use to keep it running efficiently. Cut energy use by drying clothes under the "Automatic" instead of the "Timed" setting. If you're really ready to go retro, install a clothesline in your backyard and dry your clothes for free!

Compute The Savings

Power down your computer any time you will be away from it for a long period (an hour or more.) For short breaks, use the "Sleep" or "Hibernate" modes to reduce energy use and save the time it takes to reboot.

LIGHTING

The Lights Are On And Nobody's Home

Don't overlook the obvious: turn off lights when you leave a room. Use the minimum amount of outdoor security lights and be sure they are set on a timer or motion sensor so that they turn off during the day.

Clean and Bright

Dirty bulbs don't give off as much light. Get out that dust rag and clean 'em off.

WATER HEATERS

Turn It Down

Set the thermostat on your water heater to 120 degrees. The lower temperature will protect your children from scalding at the tap while saving you energy and money. You can also try using a tankless point of use water heater. (See Chapter 2: Water, Water, Everywhere for more information.)

Bundle Up

If you have an older water heater, keep it bundled up with a blanket or insulating jacket to trap heat inside the tank. Be sure to leave openings around electrical connections, thermostats, heating elements, and drain valves.

Homemade Energy?

Once reserved only for the most ardent environmentalists, alternative energy from solar, wind, or water power is becoming easier and more cost efficient for the rest of us to use. Solar energy is a good bet for those who have the space and live in the right climate. Solar water heaters, in particular, are a simple and cost-effective way to cut your energy bill without a lot of fuss. Small, family-style wind turbines are also increasing in popularity for those who live in windy areas.

● ●

Interview with Green Parent Timberly Whitfield

If anyone knows what it's like to grow up green, it's Timberly Whitfield. At the age of six, Timberly moved with her family from a cushy life in the United States to a less-than-cushy life in Africa as United Methodist missionaries. For the next twelve years, Timberly lived in both Tanzania and Nigeria, growing up as an average African kid, with few of the luxuries (like water and electricity) that we often take for granted. She is currently the host of the daily television series "New Morning" on the Hallmark Channel and a noted public speaker on media and the environment. I caught up with Green Parent Timberly Whitfield at the Green Festival in Washington, D.C., where she shared her thoughts with me on growing up green and being a role model to the next generation.

Q: *What was your childhood like in Africa?*

A: I really grew up like a "Green Kid," although we didn't use that term. We didn't know we were green. It was just the natural way that we lived. We were environmentally conscious because of our lifestyle and the country's limited resources. All of the food that we ate came directly from the Earth, no chemicals or pesticides. We had to conserve water. I can remember as a kid having to bathe with two pitchers of water because that was all we had. We collected rainwater that came off of our roof and pumped it to drink. We had to conserve electricity, so we could only use it for three hours a night. We even had to take turns going out and hand-cranking the generator (a scary task for a little girl). When it came to washing clothes we were pretty high-tech. We had an old, old Maytag wringer type washing machine and we would fill it with one basin of water. Then we'd start with the whites, then the colors, pastels, and darks. We washed all of the clothes in the same water. At then end, we took the water (which was basically just dirt by then) and we would throw that on the garden. Everything was recycled and reused. Nothing got thrown away. These ideas are all fashionable now, but that was just the way we lived. It was difficult for me at first, because I was an American kid, but I got used to it and got the hang of it.

Q: *How would you compare your childhood with the life your daughter has now?*

A: Night and day! I hope and I plan for her to visit Africa with me one day and see how I grew up. She's heard some of the stories but she's only five so she's still a little young to understand it all. Right now she's just a typical American kid. She has a room full of toys, most of which she doesn't play with, and she still wants more. But I try to instill in her some of the things that I learned growing up. One thing that I like is that my mom has started a little project with my daughter where they go into her room and go through all of the toys, games and dolls that she is no longer playing with. She has a little bit of a hard time with it. I'm not saying it's easy. But my daughter has to try to figure out what she can part with. And then she and my mom put a box together and they go to the post office and send it to Africa.

It was really wonderful one day when we got a letter back from a mom in Africa who sent a picture of her twin girls wearing some of my daughter's clothes and holding some of her dolls. It was a touching moment because my daughter really got the connection that the girls in the picture needed something that she no longer wanted and instead of throwing it away we were able to give it to someone who was really happy to have it.

Q: *You're speaking tomorrow (at the Green Festival) about the role of the environment in minority communities. Why do you think this is a particular concern?*

A: The environment is not really a priority in minority neighborhoods because people are concerned about so many other things like unemployment and education. But I think it is important that minority leaders in the church and in the community add the environment to their platform because it does affect all people and I think if folks knew just how it does affect them and their children, then they would become a lot more involved.

Q: *What advice do you have for parents who are trying to raise their children to be environmentally conscious?*

A: Parents are role models. Period. You can talk and talk and talk, but it goes in one ear and out the other. But your kids are always watching you, so you have to set the tone. If you're recycling and conserving, I think it will get passed on and you won't have to lecture or preach. It will just come naturally.

Greensourcing

Green Power: Depending upon where you live, you may now have the option to choose your own energy supplier. If so, seek out a company that uses renewable sources of power such as solar, wind, low-impact hydroelectric, or geothermal. In some areas, you may also be able to purchase renewable energy credits (RECs) that offset your energy use by supporting renewable energy programs. Be sure to look for a reliable program like Green-e (www.green-e.org), a non-profit group that verifies and certifies RECs.

Get The Kids Involved

- **Energy Report Cards:** Help your child give his classroom (or school) an "Energy Report Card." He can audit the classroom's energy use and identify energy-efficient improvements.

- **Light Patrol:** Even the youngest children can help you remember to turn the lights off when you leave a room. Make your child responsible for "light patrol" and give him the power to reduce your household's energy consumption.

- **The Ribbon Test:** On a windy day, give your child a lightweight piece of yarn or ribbon and help her test your windows and doors for leaks. Hold the ribbon near the windowsills or door jamb. If it's fluttering, you have a leak.

- **Show Him The Light:** If your child is permanently "plugged in" to one electrical device or another, consider giving him a solar-powered charger to charge up his laptop, video games, PDA, cell phone, or iPod (See **Use Your Green** in this chapter).

• **Build A Solar Oven:** Check out Recycle Works for instructions on building a solar oven out of a pizza box (**www.recycleworks.org/schools/solar_ ovens.html**). Be sure to bake some cookies in it as a reward for your eco-savvy efforts!

U$e Your Green

ENERGY STAR Appliances: Replace worn out appliances with newer models that meet the ENERGY STAR efficiency criteria. There are more than 50 different categories of products that are eligible for the ENERGY STAR label, including battery chargers, dehumidifiers, ceiling fans, dish-washers, televisions, cordless phones, computers, printers, and even windows and doors. Look for the star before making your next purchase (www.energystar.gov).

Energy Monitors: Similar in appearance to your household thermostat, an energy monitor, like the Meter Reader from Energy Monitoring Technologies (www.energymonitor.com), can help you cut your energy use by giving you a visual, indoor display of the amount and cost of energy that you are using throughout your home.

CFL Bulbs: General Electric (www.ge.com) is the market leader, producing 60% of the compact fluorescents on store shelves today. You can now find CFLs at mass retailers everywhere.

Solar-Powered Chargers: Consider purchasing a solar-powered battery charger to power up your camera, cell phone, iPod, or laptop. Sundance Solar (http://store.sundancesolarcorp.com) makes a series of foldable solar battery chargers that are small enough to fit in a backpack. Solio (www.solio.com) and Solar Style (www.solarstyle.com) also make affordable options.

Resources

Alternative Energy Information
> American Wind Energy Association
>> windmail@awea.org
>> ww.awea.org

> Solar Energy International
>> (970) 963-8855
>> sei@solarenergy.org
>> www.solarenergy.org

> Solar Living Institute
>> (707) 744-2017
>> www.solarliving.org

> U.S. Department of Energy
>> Energy Efficiency and Renewable Energy
>> www.eere.energy.gov

Energy Auditors
> CHEERS
>> California Home Energy Rating Services
>> (800) 4-CHEERS
>> www.cheers.org
>> info@cheers.org

RESNET
Residential Energy Services Network
(760) 806-3448
info@natresnet.org
www.resnet.us

Energy Conservation Information
Home Energy Saver
http://hes.lbl.gov/hes/
Natural Resource Defense Council
(212) 727-2700
www.nrdc.org
nrdcinfo@nrdc.org

U.S. Department of Energy
1-800-dial-DOE
www.energy.gov

U.S. Environmental Protection Agency
ENERGY STAR Program
(888) STAR-YES
www.energystar.gov

Using a scrap of yarn, ribbon, or extra diaper pin, your child can have his or her very own "Light Patrol" badge.

Chapter 2:
Water, Water, Everywhere

Why is it necessary to conserve water when there is water, water every-where? Contrary to appearances, fresh water is not really as plentiful as you might think. Ninety-seven percent of the water on the planet is actually salt water, not suitable for consumption. Only 3% of the Earth's water supply is fresh, and the majority of that is locked away in ice caps and glaciers. The reality is that just 1% of the water on Earth is available for all of the world's agricultural, manufacturing, sanitation, and personal household needs.

Each American uses roughly 100-150 gallons of water on a daily basis. Inside the house, the bathroom is the biggest water drain, accounting for ¾ of all indoor water use. Outside, it's lawn care and car washing that suck up most of the water.

You pay for water three times: to buy it, to heat it (for hot water), and to take it away. So, reducing water consumption can save you a bundle on your water, energy, and sewer bills. It also eases the burden on water treatment facilities, curbing pollution and conserving energy. Here's how you can do it:

Top 5 Ways To Make An Impact

1. **Think:** It's easy to waste water when you are not thinking about it and just as easy to conserve it by paying closer attention to how and when you turn on the tap.

2. **Don't Be A Drip:** Even a small leak can waste a ton of water. A leak of just one drop per second wastes 2,700 gallons of water a year. Get out a wrench and put a stop to those drips. Not sure if your toilet is leaking? Drop a little food coloring in your toilet tank. If the color seeps into the toilet bowl without flushing, you have a leak.

3. **Do Double Duty:** Get more out of your water use by multi-tasking. Think of ways to use the same water more than once while grooming, cleaning, washing dishes, and playing. (For example, let your kids play in the sprinkler while you water the lawn.)

4. **Get Gadgets:** Faucet aerators and low-flow shower heads pay back their investment by reducing water, energy and sewer bills.

5. **Collect:** Don't put water down the drain if it can be used to water a plant or clean the car.

Green Tips

AROUND THE HOUSE

Air Conditioners

If you already have an evaporative air conditioner, direct the water run-off to a flower bed or the base of a tree. Or, consider installing an air-to-air heat pump on your air conditioning system to stay cool without wasting water.

In An Emergency

Make sure you know how and where to turn off your water quickly if a pipe were to burst. This could save thousands of gallons of water and thousands of dollars in damage to your home.

BATHROOM

Go Low Flow

Water-saving shower heads or flow restrictors can save as much as 500 to 800 gallons of water per month. Installing one takes only a few minutes, and for a small investment of $10 to $20 (some municipalities even give them away for free. Check with your county or other local resources first), you could save $50 to $75 per year on water bills and $20 to $50 or more per year on energy bills. New models do more than just block the flow of water. They are designed to aerate water, giving you a robust shower that is comparable to standard models. If you are building a new house or remodeling, consider installing a low-flow toilet that can reduce indoor water use by 20%.

Save Water While You Brush/Shave/and Lather

Old habits are hard to break, but letting the water run while you're grooming is a good one to change. Turn the water off while you brush your teeth and you will save 4 gallons a minute. That's 200 gallons a week for a family of four! Save 3 gallons of water each day by turning off the water while shaving. Instead, fill the bottom of the sink with a few inches of water to rinse your razor. In the shower, turn off the water while you shampoo and condition your hair and you can save more than 50 gallons a week. Do double duty by brushing your teeth in the shower.

Waiting For Hot Water?

Do you have a faucet or shower that takes forever to produce hot water? This is often the case when water has to travel a distance through plumbing to reach its destination. But a lot of water gets wasted while you're waiting for your shower to heat up. Consider installing a point of use water heater to produce instant hot water right where and when you need it (See **Use Your Green** in this chapter). Some states and localities offer rebates and tax incentives for installing this device.

In the meantime, don't let the cold water go down the drain. Instead, capture it with a cup or watering can to use later on house plants or your garden. This can save anywhere from 200 to 300 gallons of water each month. For baths, plug the drain before turning the water on and adjust the temperature as the tub fills up.

Double Up

If you have little children (and they aren't too dirty), bathe them together or one right after the other to save bathwater. For parents, you may not have the option to "share" a shower with the kids around, but you can still shower one right after another so that you don't have to wait for the water to heat up.

Toilet Dams

You only need about 2 gallons of water to successfully flush your toilet (older model toilets use 7-10 gallons while newer models use 3-5.) Fill a plastic water bottle with pebbles or water and place it in your toilet tank to create a "toilet dam" that cuts down on the amount of water flushed down the drain. If you have an active toilet, this can save you roughly 300 gallons of water each month.

Use Your Trash Can

Toss dead bugs, tissues, and baby wipes (even the flushable ones) in the trash can instead of the toilet to avoid unnecessary flushes.

KITCHEN

The Dirt On Dishes

Finally, some good news: A recent study conducted by the wonderful folks at the University of Bonn in Germany found that washing dishes with a dishwasher uses $\frac{1}{2}$ the energy, $\frac{1}{6}$ the water, and much less soap than washing them by hand. They even accounted for washing half loads and particularly dirty loads. Of course, your best bet is to run the dishwasher with a full load to maximize water and energy efficiency.

If you do like to go "old school" and wash your dishes by hand, minimize running water by filling one sink with soapy water and one with rinse water. If you only have one sink, use a spray device or short blasts from the tap to rinse.

Thirsty?

Keep a bottle or a pitcher of drinking water in the refrigerator. This way you won't have to run the tap to get a cool drink.

The Big Chill

Defrosting your meat or veggies with tap water can waste 100 gallons of water each month. Plan ahead and defrost food in the fridge or use the microwave when time is short.

Clean Those Veggies

Wash your fruits and veggies in a small pot rather than a stream of running water. When you finish, toss the rinse water on a houseplant.

Get More From Your Garbage

Skip the garbage disposal (they need a lot of water to operate properly). Instead, consider starting a compost pile to get rid of food waste. (See Chapter 5: How Green is Your Yard?)

LAUNDRY

Green Your Machine

Laundry machines typically have variable water settings, so if you just have a small load, set the water on its lowest setting. When purchasing a new machine, look for a water-saving model, such as a front loading machine.

THE GREAT OUTDOORS

From The Hose

Attach an adjustable nozzle to the end of your garden hose so that you can control water volume and flow. Winterize outdoor spigots when temperatures dip below freezing to prevent leaks or burst pipes. (Check out **Chapter 5: How Green is Your Yard?** for more tips on saving water in your yard.)

A Clean Ride

Time to wash that filthy car? You will actually use less water at a car wash than you would at home. Commercial car washes use high-powered hoses and recycle wash water to maximize water conservation. If you want to do the job at home, use a bucket of water to soap up the car followed by a quick rinse with the hose. If you can, make the water do double duty by washing the car on your lawn so that your grass gets a drink as well.

Dirty Sidewalk?

Save hundreds of gallons of water by using a broom instead of a hose to clean driveways and sidewalks.

For The Pool

If you have a pool, use a pool cover to cut down on evaporation. An uncovered standard-sized (16 ft. x 32 ft.) pool loses approximately an inch of water each week to evaporation. Mark the water level with a grease pencil so that you can closely monitor for leaks. Also, consider installing a water-saving pool filter.

At The Store

Did you know that it takes 1,800 gallons to make a pair of jeans, 1,000 gallons of water to make a loaf of bread, 400 gallons of water to make one cotton t-shirt, and 48 gallons of water to produce 8 fluid ounces of milk? Water is a primary ingredient in the manufacturing of almost all of your favorite stuff, so reducing your overall consumption can help to conserve water as effectively as shutting off your household tap.

Greensourcing

BYOB: Think again before purchasing bottled water. Bottled water uses more energy and resources in its production and shipping than tap water, and it is often of similar or lesser quality. Americans throw away roughly 22 million water bottles each year, swallowing up landfill as well as resources. And according to the Natural Resource Defense Council's four-year study on the bottled water industry, water that comes from a bottle is no cleaner or safer than water that comes from the tap. In fact, their study found that at least 25% of bottled water is actually just tap water in a bottle[1]. Save money and resources by carrying your own reusable bottle filled with tap water instead.

Get The Kids Involved

- **Put Some Muscle In It:** Teach your kids to put some oomph into it when they are turning off the faucet. Even little drips send a lot of water down the drain.

- **Keep 'Em Cool:** When the kids want to cool off, use the sprinkler in an area where your lawn needs it the most so that the water does double duty for entertainment and for the plants. If your child enjoys playing with the hose, let him water the garden and make sure he understands the importance of conservation.

- **Read:** Children will love *The Magic School Bus: At The Waterworks*, by Joanna Cole. It's a silly story about a trip through the fresh water cycle that will give your child a better understanding of how her water gets to the faucet.

- **Give Him Some Perspective:** Check out The Ryan's Well Foundation (www.ryanswell.ca), founded by first-grader Ryan Hrelijac, an organization that aims to raise awareness and funds for children in other countries who do not have access to clean water.

U$e Your Green

Toilets: If you have an older toilet, consider purchasing Athena's Controllable Flush Replacement Handle (www.athenacfc.com). This little beauty allows you to turn any toilet into a dual flush system. Pull the handle up to flush with your tank's full capacity (for bigger jobs); pull down to use only 1.5 gallons (for those who don't like to "let it mellow"). Athena estimates that a family of four can save over 30,000 gallons of water with this device.

Low-Flow Shower Heads: Gaiam's "Lowest Flow Shower Head" (www.gaiam.com) uses 2.25 gallons of water per minute. Bricor (www.bricor.com) makes a shower head that uses 1 gallon of water per minute and features a pause button to reduce flow further. The Aqua Helix (www.aquahelix.net) shower head squeezes out only ½ gallon per minute.

Faucet Aerators: Faucet aerators are inexpensive little gadgets that often cost under $1 while reducing your water consumption at the sink by as much as 50%. If your faucet already has an aerator installed, it will have its flow rate imprinted on the side. Look for faucets with a rate of 2.75 gallons per minute or lower. If your faucet doesn't already have an aerator, you can install your own as long as the inside tip of the faucet is threaded. You can find faucet aerators at any local plumbing or hardware store, but call your water utility company first as they may give them out for free. Online, check out Niagara Conservation at www.niagaraconservation.com.

ENERGY STAR Appliances: ENERGY STAR appliances do more than just cut down your energy bill. Dishwashers and clothes washers that meet the criteria also help you reduce your water and sewer bills. For instance, most qualified washing machines use only 18-25 gallons of water per load, compared to the 40 gallons used by a traditional model (www.energystar.gov).

Point Of Use Water Heaters: If it takes a long time for the hot water to reach your bathroom or kitchen, consider installing a point of use water heater from Ariston (www.boschhotwater.com) that produces instant hot water right where you need it and eliminates the need to run water until it is hot.

Water Savers: The AQUS™ Water System from Water Saver Technologies (www.watersavertech.com) is a cool new gadget that collects the greywater from your sink and sends it over to your toilet tank to be used in the next flush. It fits directly under your vanity and can hold up to 5½ gallons of water.

Resources

Earth 911
http://earth911.org

H2OUSE
www.h2ouse.org

Natural Resource Defense Council
(212) 727-2700
nrdcinfo@nrdc.org
www.nrdc.org

U.S. Environmental Protection Agency
ENERGY STAR Program
(888) STAR-YES
www.energystar.gov

Water Conserve
www.waterconserve.org

Water–Use It Wisely
www.wateruseitwisely.com

Chapter 3:
Talking Trash

According to the U.S. Environmental Protection Agency, each American generates about 4½ pounds of garbage each day. So, in my family of four, we are tossing away over 17 pounds of milk cartons, coloring books, juice boxes, broken dolls, toy packaging, torn-up clothes, Ziploc bags, and leftover sandwiches on a daily basis. Now that's rubbish!

Just what's in all of that garbage? The three biggies in the landfill are paper and cardboard (34%), yard trimmings (13%), and food scraps (12%). The good news is that these items are also some of the easiest to keep out of the trash can. And reducing trash even a little bit can make a huge difference. Each item you keep out of the garbage prevents emissions of greenhouse gases, reduces pollutants, saves energy, conserves resources, and reduces the need for new landfills and incinerators. It also saves you money in garbage removal costs.

The strategy for reducing trash is simple, and you've probably heard it a thousand times: reduce, reuse, and recycle. If you're like most folks, you think of recycling as the key component in reducing trash, but that should actually be your last resort. For example, if you buy water by the gallon, you can toss the plastic jugs in the recycle bin. That's good, but you can easily do better. Use a water filter and reusable containers to eliminate the waste altogether.

Top 5 Ways To Make An Impact

1. **Leave It At The Store:** The best way to reduce waste is to keep it from coming home with you in the first place. Think twice before making a purchase to determine if you really, really need it. Try this old money saving trick: leave the item at the store and promise yourself that if you really need it, you will pick it up the next time you shop.

2. **Go Paperless:** Think twice before you hit that PRINT button. Read documents, news, and magazines online. Pay bills over the web to save paper from bills and checks. Send out e-cards to save both paper and cash. At work, distribute memos and circulate documents by email.

3. **Make A Waste-Free Lunch:** Many parents rely heavily on pre-packaged and disposable goods when packing lunches. Sure, they're convenient, but what is the cost of this convenience? Much of the trash generated in the American home comes from the packaging on the food we buy. According to the website Wastefreelunches.org, each school-age child who packs a disposable lunch generates 67 pounds of waste per school year. That works out to 18,760 pounds of lunch waste for just one average-size elementary school. Ditch those pre-packaged goods and make your kids a waste-free lunch (See below for tips).

4. **Grasscycle:** Bagging up leaves and other yard trimmings not only wastes your time and energy, it also puts a tremendous strain on the

environment when it winds up in a landfill. Instead, try grasscycling. Leave grass clippings on your lawn where they will naturally decompose and hold in soil moisture, prevent freezing, and return nutrients to the soil.

5. **Recycle:** OK, if you've already bought it and you can't reuse it, the next best thing is to recycle it. Recycling is a great idea, but when you're pressed for time, it may seem just so much easier to toss things in the trash. Let's face it, when you're trying to clean up the dinner dishes, help your kids with their homework, and put up a load of laundry, it can be a real drag to rinse out that empty jar of spaghetti sauce or can of soup. Keep this in mind: Recycling creates jobs, saves energy, preserves natural resources, reduces greenhouse-gas emissions, and keeps toxins from leaking out of landfills. Recycling makes a difference!

Green Tips

REDUCE YOUR RUBBISH

Be Picky About Packaging

If you have a choice between two products, go for the one with less packaging so that you will have less to throw away when you get it home. Also, seek out a product with packaging that can be reused for other purposes at home (a box that can later be used to ship a package or cardboard that will make an interesting art project).

Choose Reusable Over Disposable

Steer clear of disposable products such as batteries, plates, cups, razors, and pens. Use reusable, rechargeable, or refillable products instead.

Consider "Preloved"

When you do make purchases, consider purchasing a gently used or "preloved" item to keep it out of the landfill and reduce the use of virgin materials.

Go Back For Seconds

At the dinner table, get in the habit of taking smaller portions and going back for seconds if you are still hungry. This strategy is not only good for your waistline; it will also significantly reduce the amount of food wasted.

Don't Buy It... Borrow Instead

Start a toy exchange with friends. As every parent knows, today's favorite toy is tomorrow's closet clutter. Instead of buying new toys every week, bring a box of your old toys to a friend's house and bring a box of their old toys home. Swap them back after a few weeks. Instead of buying books, movies, and magazines, utilize your local library or movie rental store.

Stop Junk Mail

Every time you order something online, fill out a warranty card or join a club, your personal information is collected and sold to marketers who will flood your mailbox with offers, wasting paper as well as your time. To stop junk mail, start by contacting the Mail Preference Service to request that your contact information be removed from lists run by The Direct Marketing Association (a trade group of marketing companies). Removing your information from this mailing list will cost $1, but it will also help to stop junk mail for up to five years. This can be done online at http://www.dmaconsumers.org/offmailinglist.html, or by sending a postcard or letter to: Mail Preference Service

Direct Marketing Association

P.O. Box 643

Carmel, NY 15012-0643

Credit card offers are another big source of junk mail. Call **1-888-5 OPT OUT** (or 1-888-567-8688) 24 hours a day to stop any and all unsolicited credit card offers from coming your way.

HOW TO MAKE A WASTE-FREE LUNCH

Pack a greener lunch for everyone in your family by passing on disposable, single use items and opting for reusables instead (See **Use Your Green** in **Chapter 9: The Little Green Schoolhouse** for a few suggestions). Here's how to make a waste-free lunch:

Instead of:	Use:
Aluminum foil and plastic baggies	Reusable containers for sandwiches and sides
Paper napkins	Cloth napkins
Plastic utensils	Reusable silverware
Juice boxes	Refillable drink containers
Paper lunch bags	Reusable lunchbox, tote bag or cooler

WASTE NOT: REUSE OLD STUFF

Repurpose It

Keep those old toys or clothes out of the trash by finding a new life for them. Repair, refill, rebuild, or otherwise re-purpose things instead of tossing them. Get creative by using old items (such as broken toys, torn clothing, or plastic bottles) as art supplies or turn one of your old t-shirts into a child's art smock.

Turn Trash Into Cash

If it's worth something, you can make a tidy profit by selling toys, clothes, and books at a yard sale, consignment shop or on websites like Ebay (www.ebay.com) or Craigslist (www.craigslist.org). If that doesn't work, donate them to your local thrift store or use Freecycle (www.freecycle.org) to find some-one in your area who might need them. One person's junk is another's treasure.

See Double

Whether you're at home or at work, get in the habit of using both sides of a piece of paper. Kids' art projects, grocery lists, and messages can give paper a second life. Check with your child's school to see if any of your waste (such as jars, magazines, paper towel rolls, newspapers, or plastic bottles) could be used for art projects. At the store, bring along your own shopping bags; either the plastic bags from your last trip, or better yet, a reusable tote bag.

Packing Peanuts

Call the Plastic Loosefill Council at 1-800-828-2214 for a list of locations where you can drop off those plastic peanuts that you get in shipments. Most UPS Store locations accept foam packaging peanuts for reuse. Check out www.theupsstore.com for a location near you.

Turn It Around: Recycle

The Top 10 Items To Recycle

1. Aluminum

2. PET Plastic (#1)

3. Newspaper

4. Corrugated Cardboard

5. Steel Cans

6. HDPE Plastics (#2)

7. Glass

8. Magazines

9. Mixed Paper

10. Computers

Source: National Recycling Coalition[2]

WHAT CAN YOU RECYCLE?

Recycling options vary by city or county. Most areas collect office paper, cardboard, magazines, newspaper, aluminum, plastics, glass (colored or clear), steel, yard trimmings, tires, batteries, and building materials. According to the National Recycling Coalition, here are the "Top 10" items you should always recycle.

1. Aluminum

Americans use 200 million aluminum beverage cans every day. There are no labels, covers or lids on these cans, so they are 100% recyclable. Making new aluminum cans from recycled cans uses 95% less energy than that needed to produce one from virgin ore.

2. PET Plastic Bottles (#1):

PET, or polyethylene terephthalate, is a form of polyester used to produce lightweight plastic bottles for items such as soft drinks, water, juice, liquor, cough syrup, tennis balls and cleaning products. These bottles make up 48% of the plastic bottles used in the United States. Once recycled, PET bottles can be used to make new plastic containers, sweaters, shoes, luggage, upholstery, and carpeting, as well as fiberfill for sleeping bags and coats and fabric for T-shirts and tote bags.

3. Newspaper

Compared to the production of virgin newspaper, recycled newspaper saves trees, cuts energy use by over 50%, and creates 74% less air pollution. Newspapers are easily recycled back into newsprint or into other papers, such as boxboard or newsletter stock.

4. Corrugated Cardboard

Over 90% of all products in the United States are shipped in corrugated cardboard boxes. These bulky boxes take up a lot of space in dumpsters. Recycled corrugated cardboard is used to make chipboard, boxboard (i.e., cereal boxes), paper towels, tissues, and printing paper.

5. Steel Cans

According to the U.S. Energy Information Administration (EIA), the average family in the United States uses 90 pounds of steel cans a year. The EIA estimates that recycling that steel would save 144 kilowatt hours of electricity, 63 pounds of coal, 112 pounds of iron, and 5.4 pounds of limestone. Today, all steel products are made with at least some recycled steel.

6. HDPE Plastic Bottles (#2)

HDPE, or high density polyethylene, plastics account for 47% of all plastic bottles consumed in the United States. These stiff, impact resistant bottles are often used to hold products such as milk and laundry detergent. Once recycled, they are easily converted into new bottles or plastic pipe.

7. Glass Containers

Glass is used to package many food products such as juices, jellies, baby food, and vegetable oils. It currently makes up about 5% of the trash that hits the landfills. Recycled glass is easily made into new glass jars and bottles or into other glass products like fiberglass insulation. And, unlike paper, glass products can be recycled over and over again without wearing out. Using recycled glass to make new glass products requires 40% less energy than making it from virgin materials.

8. Magazines

Tons of outdated magazines and catalogs hit the landfills each year. Instead of tossing yours, donate them to local schools or day care centers for craft projects. Hospitals and doctor's offices often accept donations of recent edition magazines. Recycled magazines and catalogs can also be combined with old newspapers and wood chips to make newsprint, tissue, boxboard, and printing paper.

9. Mixed Paper

Paper products such as office paper, envelopes, telephone books, and brown bags make up about 35% of the trash in the United States, the largest single sector of waste. According to the World Resources Institute, in 2005, each person in the United States consumed 653.5 pounds of paper. That means it takes over one ton of paper and 4.3 cubic yards of landfill space to handle the yearly paper consumption for a family of four.

Recycled paper can be used to make products such as new paper, molded packaging, compost and kitty litter. Recycling paper products reduces energy consumption, decreases combustion and landfill emissions, and decreases the amount of carbon dioxide in the atmosphere.

10. Computers

Old computers and electronics are a major contributor to the waste stream. That's no surprise considering how quickly these items become outdated and obsolete. They are also difficult to dispose of because they are made up of a number of components that are toxic to the environment. Fortunately, many computers can be repaired or upgraded, extending their life by a few years. They can also be donated (with a tax deduction) and refurbished for use in local schools, charities and non-profit organizations. Earth 911 (**www.earth911.org**) maintains a list on their website of organizations that accept computer donations. As a last resort, computers can be recycled so that their components (plastics, glass, steel, gold, lead, mercury, and cadmium) can be recaptured and used again.

REACH OUT

When you're talking trash, the final step in the process is to support the recycling industry by purchasing recycled products. You can find everything from printer paper to furniture to ski jackets that are made from recycled materials. This helps increase demand for recycling and reduces the use of virgin materials and the production of new wastes.

The Great Diaper Debate

For years, new parents have been vexed in their efforts to choose an environmentally friendly diaper. Cloth diaper fans have long insisted that theirs is the better choice because cloth is reusable and therefore doesn't take up space in the landfill. Disposable diaper devotees, on the other hand, counter that disposables are more eco-friendly because they don't need to be washed and therefore save both water and energy.

Independent studies have consistently come to the conclusion that there is no significant difference in the environmental impact between disposables and cloth. So what's an eco-minded parent to do?

One alternative to consider is a new product called gDiapers (www.gdiapers.com), which combines a washable cloth pant with a biodegradable and flushable insert liner. Unlike disposable diapers, they don't use any elemental plastics or landfill space, and they require less of the water and energy used to wash standard cloth diapers. These "hybrid" diapers are good in a pinch, but they still require paper and packaging (and midnight trips to the store for refills!)

Some parents have eschewed diapers all together and turned to a method called "elimination communication" where parents learn to "read" their baby's cues and rush them to the potty when they appear ready to go. An inevitable mess aside, this method is unquestionably better for the environment because it doesn't require water, energy, or landfill space. However, it is not for the faint of heart. If you can't devote your full attention to watching your baby for "cues," save yourself and your baby some frustration and use another method.

For those who prefer a traditional diaper, cotton diapers can take the environmental edge over disposables with some energy and water saving techniques, such as line-drying, skipping the pre-soak, and washing diapers in large loads using low temperatures. And today's parents don't have to go old-school with pins and plastic pants. Cotton diapers now come in such a wide array of styles and colors, that green parents may finally be able to put an end to the great diaper debate and think about more important things— like sleep! (See **Use Your Green** for recommendations.)

Get The Kids Involved

- **Craft Challenge:** Challenge your kids to turn trash into art. A plastic water bottle or milk jug makes an excellent bird feeder, baby food jars convert easily into paperweights or snow globes, and a toilet paper tube can be transformed into a pencil holder or a napkin ring. Check out www.resourcefulschools.org for lots of ideas (learn how to make your own paper or find ten crafts to make with a paper bag). Kids can also learn to make envelopes from old magazines at www.recycleworks.org.

- **Weigh Your Waste:** Try this experiment with your children: Every night for a week, collect your household garbage and weigh it on your bathroom scale. Record your results every few weeks and celebrate your success as your trash slims down.

- **Preserve Paper:** Ask kids to get the O.K. from teachers to hand in assignments via email or on a reusable disk rather than on paper.

- **For The Science Fair:** Kids can conduct a classroom waste audit to help fellow students (and teachers) learn what goes into their trash cans and how it could be reduced. Learn how at www.recycleworks.org.

Interview with Green Parent Kathleen Ridihalgh

With a toddler at home, a full-time job at the Sierra Club, and a part-time gig as a green parenting blogger, Kathleen Ridihalgh is no stranger to juggling a busy schedule. Yet she remains passionate about protecting the environment and works hard to make eco-friendly choices for her family. Kathleen chronicles her adventures in green parenting and offers "Great Green Tips" on her blog which was recently picked up by the Seattle Post Intelligencer (http://blog.seattlepi.nwsource.com/greenparenting/index.asp). Here's what Green Parent Kathleen Ridihalgh had to say about birthday parties, organic gardening, and laser-powered diaper cleaning.

Q: *Do you find it more or less difficult to be environmentally friendly now that you are a parent?*

A: Both! It's harder because you have less time and there are so many more choices to make as a parent. It is often just easier to buy pampers and not think about it, especially when you don't have a lot of time and resources. It's also harder because it's different. Before I had my baby I was able to ride my bike to work and spend a lot of time on my organic garden. I just don't have time to do that anymore. But it is also easier because it gives you a barrier between you and the corporate culture. Some parents feel a lot of pressure to buy everything and have huge birthday parties. If you've made the choice to live more simply, you can zone out some of the pressures that seem to be very stressful for a lot of people.

Q: *What do you think is the biggest challenge facing parents who are trying to be more environmentally conscious?*

A: There are two big challenges for parents and they are both societal. One is that our country isn't really family-friendly in terms of health care and day care and support for working mothers. So many people are struggling to make ends meet that it's just not on the top of the list to figure out how they are going to recycle or cook fresh foods or wash cloth diapers everyday. That is a big challenge for people. The other problem goes back to the whole corporate consumer culture thing. I get tons of catalogs and I always have to keep reminding myself that I don't want to just buy everything. But there is a lot of pressure to spend money. Parents spend so much money on their children each year. If all of that money was used to buy recycled products or secondhand products that would be a huge power in the consumer culture.

Q: *What is your best "Great Green Tip" for parents?*

A: Buying secondhand is probably the easiest and most powerful thing people can do, because everybody's going to buy stuff for their kids. There's just no way around it. There are so many used toys, books, and clothes out there that are clean, safe, and in good shape and buying them instead of new would really cut down on the new clothes and toys and books that need to be produced. This would save an enormous amount of energy. And that's also the biggest place where people can see a savings in their own pocket. Recently, I was looking for a little slide to put in the backyard for my daughter. I went on Craigslist and there were about 30 slides that had been posted to Craigslist just in that week. And if we don't buy these things they will just go into a landfill. So it helps on that end too.

Q: *What is your dream eco-savvy product?*

A: I can't really think of a specific product, but I know it would have something to do with dirty diapers. I think the biggest challenge to people using cloth diapers is having to deal with the mess. If there was some way you could just shoot a laser at it and make it clean, more people would use cloth.

U$e Your Green

Recycled Paper: Recycled paper products can be found at stores large and small all across the country. Look for recycled paper with the highest percentage of post-consumer content (30% is good, 100% is the best). Those labeled with a certification from the Forest Stewardship Council (FSC) were produced from trees grown in sustainably managed forests. Also, look for products that have been processed without the use of polluting chlorine. They will be labeled either PCF (processed chlorine free) or TCF (totally chlorine free). Brands to look for include Mead (look for their recycled products) (**www.mead.com**), Domtar (**www.domtar.com**), Dolphin Blue (**www.dolphinblue.com**), New Leaf Paper (**www.newleafpaper.com**) and Cascades (**www.cascades.com**). This book is even printed on Cascades RollandEnviro 100 paper (that's 100% recycled/100% post-consumer waste paper!).

Recycled-Content Stuff: One of the best ways to promote recycling is to purchase products that are made from recycled materials. Yesterday's trash can be used to make everything from clothes to art. Here are just a few examples: The website Eco-artware.com (**www.eco-artware.com**) offers a dazzling selection of art made from recycled materials (my favorite is the "Good Egg Footstool" made from 100% recycled paper egg cartons). Patagonia offers a line of clothing (**http://patagonia.com/recycle**), made out of recycled duds, for men, women, and children.

Recycling Containers: If you're looking for a way to control all of those recyclables in your kitchen, consider the Ecopod (www.ecopod.org), a one stop container/compactor that holds and sorts most of your recyclables. For those with limited space, the Apartment Recycling Bag from Conserv-A-Store (www.conservastore.com) might be a good option.

Cotton Diapers: Cotton diapers are easier to use than ever before; and, let's face it, they are just way cuter than disposables. Fuzzi Bunz cotton diapers (www.fuzzibunz.com) are great-looking, ridiculously soft, and a snap (literally!) to use.

Resources

Earth 911
(480) 889-2650
www.earth911.org

National Recycling Coalition, Inc.
(202) 789-1430
info@nrc-recycle.org   www.nrc-recycle.org

U.S. Environmental Protection Agency

EPA Region 1	(ME, NH, VT, MA, RI, CT):	(888) 372-7341
EPA Region 2	(NY, NJ, PR, VI):	(212) 637-3660
EPA Region 3	(PA, DE, DC, MD, VA, WV):	(800) 438-2474
EPA Region 4	(KY, TN, NC, SC, MS, AL, GA, FL):	(800) 241-1754
EPA Region 5	(MN, WI, IL, MI, IN, OH):	(800) 621-8431
EPA Region 6	(NM, TX, OK, AR, LA):	(800) 887-6063
EPA Region 7	(NE, KS, IA, MO):	(800) 223-0425
EPA Region 8	(MT, ND, WY, SD, UT, CO):	(303) 312-6149
EPA Region 9	(CA, NV, AZ, HI):	(866) EPA-WEST
EPA Region 10	(WA, OR, ID, AK):	(800) 424-4EPA

www.epa.gov

Chapter 4:
The Green Clean

I have never been described as a neat freak. And my lack of skills in this department is precisely why I was initially hesitant to trade in my brand name cleaners for a homemade variety. Like most parents, I counted on my arsenal of traditional cleaning products to wipe up the dizzying array of juice spills, muddy footprints, craft project shrapnel, and potty training accidents.

It really wasn't that long ago that homes were cleaned using inexpensive, non-toxic, common household ingredients. Now we're lead to believe that only synthetic, pre-packaged products that are loaded with chemicals can do the job. The average American home contains roughly 63 synthetic chemical products, the majority of which are cleaning agents. Many of these products use chemicals that are extremely toxic to both the environment and human health. In fact, the very products that you use to make your home clean and safe for your family could actually be harming their health.

The good news is that it is actually easy to wean yourself from this chemical dependence. I have found that by doing so, my home is not only cleaner, but safer for my children. Here are a number of green cleaning options that even the busiest parents with the messiest kids will appreciate.

Top 5 Ways To Make An Impact

1. **DIY:** Save money and the environment by making your own cleaning agents from natural, non-toxic ingredients. (See **DIY** below for instructions and tips.)

2. **Purchase:** If you don't have the time or desire to make your own, look for non-toxic earth friendly cleaning agents the next time you shop. (See **Use Your Green** in this chapter for suggestions.)

3. **Reuse:** I know as well as any other parent that paper towels and other disposable cleaning wipes are just plain handy when it comes to cleaning up fast. But it's actually just as fast to reach for a reusable cloth to do the job. For sponges, look for natural sponges that are biodegradable and can even be composted when they are no longer useful as sponges. (Just be sure they come from a sponge farm and not a natural ecosystem.)

4. **Toss It:** If you are ready to replace your traditional cleaning products with homemade solutions, GREAT! But don't just toss the old stuff in the trash. These chemicals certainly don't belong in the home, but they also too toxic for the drain or the landfill. Check with your local community dis-posal organization to find out when and where you can dispose of these products properly.

5. **Support Green Dry Cleaners (Or skip dry cleaning all together):** Look for a dry cleaner that uses green technology such as liquid carbon dioxide, Green Earth, or "wet" cleaning. See **Greensourcing** in this chapter for more information.

Green Tips

DIY

Making your own cleaning agents will save you a fortune in cleaning supplies, simplify your cleaning routine, and go a long way towards protecting the
planet. I use simply vinegar and water to get my windows, floors, and coun-
tertops sparkling (at least until the kids come along). And a sprinkle of baking
soda is all I need to clean toilets, sinks, and bathtubs. If you want to get fancy,
try out some of these simple yet effective recipes (be careful with any products and recipes, you may want to test them in a small area first, especially
on rugs and carpets that can get stained):

All-Purpose Disinfectant: Mix 2 teaspoons borax, 4 tablespoons vinegar,
and 3 cups hot water in a spray bottle. Need to cut through kitchen counter
grime? Add ¼ teaspoon liquid soap to the mixture.

Furniture Polish: Mix a one-to-one ratio of olive oil and vinegar to clean and
polish wood furniture.

Oven cleaner: Oven cleaning is the bane of my existence, so I typically try
to avoid it by placing a cookie sheet on the bottom rack of the oven to catch
spills. But for delicate recipes, this is not always an option. You can steer
clear of toxic chemicals by using good old baking soda to clean the oven.
Simply make a paste using 1 cup of baking soda and water. Apply to grimy
spots and let stand. Lift off large deposits with a spatula and scrub surface
with a scouring pad.

Windows: Mix 3 tablespoons of vinegar with 1 quart of water in a clean spray bottle. Can't see through the handprints? Try a mix of ½ teaspoon of liquid soap, 3 tablespoons of vinegar, and 2 cups of water. And to get those windows streak-free, use newspaper rather than paper towels to wipe them clean.

Metal Cleaners: Use sliced lemons to clean the tarnish from brass, copper, bronze, and aluminum. For extra dirty jobs, sprinkle the item with baking soda and then rub with lemon. To clean sterling silver, line a plastic or glass bowl with aluminum foil. Sprinkle the foil with a little salt and baking soda and then fill the bowl with warm water. Soak silver items in this mixture and the tarnish will migrate from your silver to the aluminum foil. Rinse and dry the silver, then buff it with a soft, clean cloth.

Floors: To get floors good and clean without harmful chemicals, add 1 cup of vinegar per pail of hot water. For linoleum floors, combine ¼ cup washing soda, 1 tablespoon of liquid soap, ¼ cup vinegar, and 2 gallons hot water. This will work on everything from muddy footprints to greasy spills. But do not use this formula on waxed floors.

Tubs and Sinks: Baking soda and liquid soap can work wonders in your bathroom. Simply sprinkle baking soda on porcelain tubs and sinks. Add a little of the liquid soap to a wet cloth and use it to rub in the baking soda. Rinse the fixture well to avoid leaving a hazy film.

Toilets: Make your toilet sparkle by adding ½ cup vinegar to the toilet bowl. Allow it to sit for 30 minutes and then scrub with a toilet brush. Alternatively, sprinkle a little baking soda inside the bowl and scrub. To clean the outer surfaces, sprinkle a wet cloth with baking soda and wipe down toilet.

Drain Cleaner: Clean sink and tub drains by pouring ½ cup of baking soda down the drain, followed by 1 cup vinegar. Let the mixture sit for 15 minutes and then rinse with hot water. For tough clogs, use the same mixture but allow it to sit overnight before rinsing.

Carpeting and Rugs: Fabric flooring tends to soak up the odors of the home, whether they are related to a pet or child. To absorb odors and clean your carpet naturally, sprinkle baking soda over the surface of the carpet and let it stand for 15 to 30 minutes before vacuuming. Check out these recipes from Sierra Club Canada (**www.sierraclub.ca**) for handling heavy-duty dirt and stains[3]:

Heavy-Duty Cleaner: Make a paste from ¼ each of salt, vinegar, and borax. Rub into the spot and let dry before vacuuming.

Mud: Rub salt into the mud. Let dry for one hour and vacuum.

Chocolate: Make a paste from borax and water. Rub into the stain.

Coffee: Rub club soda into the coffee spot and wipe up with a towel or sponge.

Grease: Cover with cornstarch or cornmeal, let sit awhile, rub in and vacuum.

Red Wine: Cover the stain with salt while wet. Let dry completely, and then vacuum.

Clothing: If your clothes are not really dirty, you can simply wash them in cold or warm water to remove roughly 45% of the dirt. However, in my house, with two little ones and a dog running amok, 45% is just not going to cut it. Unfortunately, I have not yet found a DIY laundry detergent recipe that comes even close to the cleaning power of commercial detergents (most brands remove about 80%-90% of soil from clothing). But the good news is that there are a number of eco-savvy laundry detergent options (See **Use Your Green** in this chapter). Unfortunately, these greener products may be more costly, so stretch your supply with these tips:

Fabric Softener: Add ¼ cup of white vinegar during the washing machine's rinse cycle to remove odors and leave clothes soft and fresh.

Stain Remover: Soaking clothes in laundry soap for about a half hour before washing is often all you need to remove a stain. But for tough stains (think grassy knees on softball pants or your toddler's spaghetti-encrusted shirt) try using a paste made of baking soda and water. Apply to the stain and let stand for one hour before washing. For whites, try using a little lemon juice and water. Rub into the stain and let stand for one hour before washing. Hydrogen peroxide can also be used as a bleach alternative for whites.

Detergent Booster: You can cut down on the amount of laundry detergent you need to use by adding a little baking soda to boost your detergent's cleaning power. If you use a liquid detergent, add ½ cup baking soda at the beginning of the wash. For powdered detergent, add ½ cup baking soda during the rinse cycle.

Starch: Mix one heaping teaspoon of corn starch with one cup of hot water until the corn starch is completely dissolved. Pour into a spray bottle and use immediately while ironing clothes.

FRESHEN UP

You don't need a bottle of chemicals to make your home smell great. Add any one of your favorite smelling herbs such as cinnamon, cloves, or rosemary to boiling water and allow it to simmer on the stove for a few minutes to freshen the air. Indoor plants are another great way to keep indoor air fresh and clean. They won't necessarily remove odors, but they work great as air filters. And if you like your house to smell like fresh baked apple pie or chocolate chips cookies, why not make everyone happy and actually bake some?

Greensourcing

Green Cleaners: No time to do the cleaning yourself? No problem. You can still get a green clean by making sure the cleaning service you hire will either use the green products you have at home, or bring their own. There is not yet a one-stop location for finding a green cleaner in your area. Check with friends for a recommendation or talk with your current cleaning agency to see if they will comply. Also, if you are getting your carpets steam-cleaned, seek out a company that uses only water or eco-friendly solvents.

Green Dry Cleaners: Conventional dry cleaners use an industrial solvent called Perchloroethylene (PERC) which is seriously toxic to humans and a common ingredient in smog. Seek out a dry cleaner that uses environmentally friendly technology. Thanks to government regulations and increased demand, green dry cleaners are spreading. Eco-friendly dry cleaners skip the chemicals and use either liquid carbon (high pressure and liquid CO_2), Green Earth (silicone-based solvents), or "wet" cleaning (soap and water) to get clothes clean. (See Resources in this chapter for more information.)

Get The Kids Involved

- **Role Play:** Give your child a small bucket of water and a sponge and let her pretend to be Cinderella cleaning the castle. She may miss a few spots but she'll have a great time, and hey…you won't have to do it yourself! I have a friend whose four-year-old daughter begged to clean their kitchen floor every day for months (her mom was only too happy to comply!).

- **Bake:** Need to freshen up the house? Enlist your child's help in baking a batch of cookies or a pie. You will enjoy the fresh, sweet smell for hours after the treats have been devoured.

- **Clean Those Toys!:** The beauty of using non-toxic ingredients such as water or vinegar to clean your home is that even young children can handle them (with supervision, of course). So give your child a rag and spray bottle filled with warm water and a splash of vinegar and let him disinfect his train set or dolls.

U$e Your Green

Green Cleaners: The DIY alternatives listed above are not for every parent. Fortunately, increasing demand has created a flourishing market for green cleaning products that are available in local health food stores as well as national chains such as Target, Lowes, Wegmans, and, of course, Whole Foods. A truly green cleaning product will be non-toxic, biodegradable, and made from renewable resources (not petroleum). But don't just rely on the labels. Manufacturers are not required to list all the ingredients in their products, and there is not yet an industry standard to define terms such as "natural," "green," or "eco-friendly" when it comes to cleaning goods.

Companies that do disclose their full list of ingredients include Ecover (www.ecover.com), Seaside Naturals (www.seasidenaturals.com) and Seventh Generation (www.seventhgeneration.com). Actor Ed Begley, Jr. puts his name and his environmental reputation on the line with an all-purpose cleaner called Begley's Best All Purpose Cleaner (www.begleysbest.com) that is child-safe, vegan, non-toxic, non-caustic, non-allergenic, and 99% biodegradable within seven days.

Reusable Cleaning Supplies: Lighten the load on your trash can by using reusable sponges and cloths in lieu of disposable paper towels and wipes. Target (www.target.com) has a great line of organic cotton cloths and towels. Method (www.method.com) makes microfiber cloths that are specialized for a variety of surfaces (stainless steel, wood, or windows). For a new twist on cleaning, try the new line of sponges and cleaning cloths available from Twist (www.twistclean.com). All of their products are biodegradable and packaged in recyclable paper packaging that can be reused for fun craft projects (check out their website for info). And don't forget to reuse those clean cotton diapers as dust cloths once your baby is potty trained.

Resources

Green Seal
(202) 872-6400
greenseal@greenseal.org
www.greenseal.org
This non-profit agency certifies environmentally responsible products.

U.S. Environmental Protection Agency
Environmentally Preferable Cleaners
Jim Darr (202) 564-8841
darr.james@epa.gov
http://www.epa.gov/epp/pubs/products/cleaner.htm

Washington Toxics Coalition
(206) 632-1545
info@watoxics.org
www.watoxics.org

Green Dry Cleaner Directories

Earth 911
http://www.earth911.org/master.asp?s=ls&serviceid=139
A directory of "wet" cleaners

Find CO2
http://findco2.com/
A directory of CO2 dry cleaners

Green Earth Dry Cleaners
http://www.greenearthcleaning.com/rostersearch.asp
A directory of "Green Earth" dry cleaners

Chapter 5:

How Green Is Your Yard?

Every year, Americans use 10,000 gallons of water, 70 million pounds of pesticides and over $5 billion dollars worth of fertilizers in an effort to create "natural" looking lawns where our children will play. According to the U.S. Fish and Wildlife Service, "Homeowners use up to 10 times more chemical pesticides per acre on their lawns than farmers use on their crops."[4] These chemicals wreak havoc on the environment and leave a chemical residue on your lawn that is anything but safe for children.

Kids don't have to play outside to be affected. Lawn-care chemicals that are tracked indoors on kid's shoes and pet's paws can migrate all around the house. In a 2001 study published in the journal *Environmental Health Perspectives,* researchers tested indoor surfaces after the popular herbicide 2,4-D, (a known hormone disruptor) was applied to lawns. Their study found the pesticide "in indoor air and on all surfaces throughout all homes," including kitchen tables, windowsills, and floors.[5] According to the EPA, short-term exposure to high levels of 2,4-D can cause nervous system damage, while long-term exposure is also linked to kidney and liver damage.[6] Here's how to make your yard a greener place to be without using an acre of chemicals.

Top 5 Ways To Make An Impact

1. **Water Less:** Did you know that more plants die from over-watering than from under-watering? Keep that in mind the next time you reach for a hose. Only water your lawn when it needs it (it doesn't spring back when you step on it).

2. **Mow Less:** Longer grass grows deeper roots that make it stronger, healthier, and less susceptible to weed and pest infiltration. Mow your lawn less and you will not only save yourself time and sweat, you will also save the planet by reducing the need for water, fertilizers, and pesticides.

3. **Reduce Your Chemical Dependence:** Replace your toxic chemical pesticides, herbicides, and fertilizers with "greener" solutions. See the Green Tips below for more information.

4. **Choose Plants That Suit Your Area:** You can significantly reduce the amount of water and chemicals you need to use on your lawn by planning ahead with your landscaping. Xeriscaping is a scary sounding term that simply means choosing plants that are suited to the fuel moisture and soil conditions of your yard. Plants that are native to your area will survive and even thrive in your particular climate without extra effort on your part. Check with your local nursery for suggestions.

5. **Compost:** Keep your food scraps, yard waste, and newspapers out of the garbage by turning them into usable compost instead. Find out how in this chapter.

Green Tips

LANDSCAPING

Plant In Groups

Group plants together based on similar water needs to save time and avoid wasting water. For example, vegetables and bedding plants tend to have relatively shallow roots and require more frequent watering than, say, a cactus or drought-tolerant shrub like a California Lilac.

Get Your Timing Right

Timing is everything when it comes to getting a great looking yard. Plant in the spring or fall when temperatures are cooler and the water requirements for plants are lower. Your plants will have a greater chance of thriving with less work on your part.

Reduce Your Yard

Walkways and patios can help you get better use out of your yard while adding value to your property and reducing the amount of yard that needs to be maintained and watered.

Cover It Up

Heavy mulching around trees, shrubs, and flower beds helps to control weeds, reduce evaporation, and maintain more consistent soil temperature.

WATERING

Less But More

As a rule of thumb, it's best to water your plants deeply but less frequently to encourage strong, healthy plants. When plants receive frequent bursts of water, they focus on top growth rather than driving down roots. Deep watering promotes deep root growth and healthier plants that look great with less attention from you.

Maximize Your Efforts

Water in the cool, early morning hours to prevent evaporation and maximize your watering efforts. Watering in the evening is fine, too, but may lead to the development of fungus. Skip watering on windy days when you are more likely to water your fence than your yard. Water hanging baskets and potted plants by placing an ice cube under the dirt. For gardens and flower beds, consider using soaker hoses or drip irrigation systems to make water conservation easy.

Give It A Sprinkle

If you use a sprinkler, look for one that delivers large drops of water close to the ground, as mist sprays are more likely to evaporate. Set a kitchen timer so that you don't forget to turn off the water. Turn off sprinklers when it's raining or install a rain shut-off device to do it automatically. Also, check your sprinklers regularly to make sure they are watering your lawn and not your driveway or sidewalk. For steep slopes, use a soaker hose or water in timed intervals to prevent wasteful runoff.

MOWING

Maintain Your Mower

Save energy (yours and the planet's) by making sure your lawn mower is in good working order. Sharpen the blades and set them one notch higher. This will allow grass to grow just a smidge taller to shade out weeds and hold onto moisture.

Weeds and Critters

Weeds and pests compete with your plants for food and water, so you'll need to get rid of them to keep your plants healthy. But there is no need to reach for chemicals that are harmful to your children, pets, and the environment when natural alternatives are just as effective. Here are some natural organic remedies that can be used to rid your lawn of weeds and critters. Also, check out **Use Your Green** in this chapter for a list of companies that offer non-toxic, organic lawn care products.

Liquid Soap: Soap works wonders at eliminating aphids, sawflies, spider mites, scale, whiteflies, and wasps. Mix 2 tablespoons of liquid soap with 1 gallon of water in a spray bottle. Alternatively, mix 1 cup vegetable oil (such as corn or safflower) with one tablespoon dish soap and 1 gallon of water and spray on plants.

Vinegar: Regular, household vinegar is an effective herbicide that can kill weeds without harming the environment. However, be sure to use it sparingly and only in areas where you don't want anything to grow as it will kill any plant in its path (from dandelions to your prized roses.)

Hot Pepper: Combine ½ cup hot pepper with 2 cups of water in your blender and spray on garden plants to detract pests such as cucumber beetles, tomato hornworms, and caterpillars.

Corn Gluten: Corn gluten is a non-toxic by-product of milling corn that kills weed seedlings and adds nitrogen to the soil. It only works on plants before they sprout, so it's safe to use on existing grass. It is especially effective against crabgrass.

Bacillus thuringiensis: This bacterium, also known as Bt, can be added to your garden in powder or spray form to attack garden pests.

Beer: To get rid of slugs and snails, fill a small dish with beer to attract the pests and drown them.

Plants: Check with your local garden center to learn more about plants that you can use to naturally protect your garden. For instance, daisies will attract wasps that eat beetles.

FERTILIZERS

Rather than raking up grass clippings after you mow, leave them on your yard to return nutrients to the soil. This is especially useful if you have clover in your yard as this legume adds rich nitrogen to the soil (so you don't need to use a chemical fertilizer). In the fall, ditch the rake and mow leaves into usable compost to feed your lawn. If you have a fish tank, pour the nutrient-rich water into your garden every time you clean it out. One of the best all-natural fertilizers is organic compost. You can purchase it at the store or make your own from yard trimmings and kitchen waste.

How To Start Your Own Compost Pile

Compost is the ultimate recycler, turning your yard waste and kitchen scraps into usable mulch that you can use to feed your plants. It's as eco-friendly as you can get. And the best part about it is that it is cheap, and after the initial set-up it is relatively easy to do. There are many resources you can use to learn more about composting, but here are the basics:

A successful compost pile needs two basic components: carbon (shredded newspapers, cardboard, and straw) and nitrogen (lawn clippings, kitchen waste, and weeds).

Combine these components in a ratio of roughly 5 parts carbon to 1 part nitrogen in a compost bin or pile in your yard.

Feeling lazy? Leave the pile alone and you will have usable compost by next year. In a rush? Turn the pile and add a sprinkle of water every few weeks and your compost will be ready in about three months (See **Use Your Green** for a compost bin that makes composting a breeze).

Greensourcing

Green Lawn Care: If you hire out your lawn care, you can still keep it green by making sure the company or individual you choose under-stands organic yard care. Check out the websites for Beyond Pesticides (www.beyondpesticides.org) or The Northeast Organic Farming Association (www.nofa.org) to find an accredited "green" specialist in your area.

Get Your Kids Involved

- **Plant A Memory:** Plant a tree or a garden together and you will create a memory that will last even after the leaves have fallen. Caring for a plant of their own is a great way for kids to learn about caring for the earth. Work together to pick out a tree that is well suited to your soil type and climate. Or, choose a few vegetables that your child can monitor throughout the growing season. You'll be amazed at how excited kids are to eat veggies when they had a hand in growing them!

- **Decomposition Detective:** Help your kids understand composting by making a small pile that they can track. Using a bucket or a small area in your yard, have your child bury compostable food scraps from your last meal under a layer of soil. Leave the scraps buried and undisturbed for one week, then have your child unearth the pile and monitor its decomposition progress.

- **Get Wiggly:** Vermicomposting is an excellent way to teach kids about ecology while turning your food scraps into usable compost. Using worms (typically red wigglers), vermicomposting processes organic food into nutrient-rich soil. You can start with a small bin (such as a 12-gallon plastic tub) and a pound of worms, or go larger if you have a big family (and lots of scraps). Check out Kids Recycle! (www.kidsrecycle.org) for a guide to resources on vermicomposting.

U$e Your Green

Gardening Supplies: Check with your local nursery to find earth-friendly gardening supplies, such as organic compost and fertilizer, and all-natural herbicides and pesticides. Planet Natural (**www.planetnatural.com**) and Gardener's Supply Company (**www.gardeners.com**) are two online sources.

Rain Barrels: With a little ingenuity, you can collect rain water for watering your plants in anything that will hold water (with a mesh screen on top to prevent the breeding of mosquitoes). If you want to get technical, surf over to The Center For Watershed Protection (**www.cwp.org**) and search for "rain barrel" for instructions on building and installing a rain barrel using a 55-gallon drum. For the pre-made variety, browse your local garden supply store, or try Clean Air Gardening (**www.cleanairgardening.com**).

Compost Bins: The size compost bin that you need will be determined by your expectations and dedication to the project, as there are bins in all shapes and sizes. You can build your own with a couple of boards or a wire cage. If you decide to purchase one, check out the Back Porch Compost Tumbler, available through Planet Natural (**www.planetnatural.com**). It doesn't take up a lot of space, won't look unsightly in your yard, lets you "roll" the compost (rather than turn it with a shovel), and it can produce finished compost in 4-6 weeks. Also check out the Rolypig composter. It looks like a pig, and you "feed" the waste into a snout, and the compost comes out of the rear! It doesn't get much easier than that!

Resources

Beyond Pesticides
(202) 543-5450
info@beyondpesticides.org
www.beyondpesticides.org

Compost Guide
www.compostguide.com

How To Compost
www.howtocompost.org

Kids Recycle!
Vermi-Composting Resources
http://www.kidsrecycle.org/worms.php

Northeast Organic Farming Association
Bill Duesing
(203) 888-5146
bduesing@cs.com
www.nofa.org

Organic Gardening
www.organicgardening.com

Pesticide Action Network
(415) 981-1771
panna@panna.org
www.panna.org

The National Pesticide Information Center
(800) 858-7378
npic@ace.orst.edu
www.npic.orst.edu

U.S. Environmental Protection Agency
   Basic Information on Composting
   www.epa.gov/compost/basic.htm
   GreenScapes Program
   www.epa.gov/greenscapes

Chapter 6:
Eco-Pets

Does your home accommodate critters of the hairy, feathered, or scaled variety? According to the Humane Society, there are currently 73 million dogs and 90 million cats in homes across the United States. Birds, bunnies, ferrets, and lizards are other popular pets for children. The food, toys, and bedding for these pets (and even the pets themselves) have a significant impact on the environment. Here's how to reduce your pet's ecological paw print.

Top 5 Ways To Make An Impact

1. **Adopt:** There are over 5,500 puppies and kittens (compared with 415 human babies) born every hour in the United States. According to the Humane Society of the United States (**www.hsus.org**), animal shelters take in between 6–8 million dogs and cats every year, of which 3–4 million are euthanized. Why buy a dog or cat when you can adopt one from your local animal shelter for a fraction of the cost?

Check out **www.petfinder.com** to find your next dog, cat, bird, rabbit or reptile friend. If you're looking for a specific breed, contact the Human Society (See **Resources** in this chapter) to locate a purebred rescue group in your area.

2. **Spay Or Neuter:** Spaying and neutering reduces this overpopulation. It also helps dogs and cats live longer by eliminating the possibility of uterine, ovarian, and testicular cancer, and decreasing the incidence of prostate disease. Check with your local animal shelter to see if they offer a free or low-cost service.

3. **Go Organic:** It may seem pretentious to purchase organic pet food for your furry friend (who is content to lick his nether regions and drink from curbside puddles), but the crops and livestock raised to produce Fido's food can be just as harsh on the environment and on your pet as the food we humans eat. See **Feed 'Em the Good Stuff** below for more information.

4. **Seek Simple Pleasures:** Look for simple, eco-friendly toys for your pet. Dogs love to chase and chew sticks of any kind. Cats and rabbits might enjoy leftover boxes and bags from your holiday wrapping, pine cones from the backyard, or a paper bag.

5. **Give Kitty Some Jingle Bells:** Keep your kitty indoors to protect her overall health and that of the environment. Cats are keen hunters and are a leading cause of death for birds, second only to habitat destruction. If your feline loves to roam, put a bell on her collar to keep her out of mischief and give the birds a flying chance.

Green Tips

Stuff It

No, I am not suggesting that you have your favorite pet stuffed. But I am suggesting that you resist the temptation to purchase a pet as a toy for your child. Yes, your little one loved the little chick she saw at the farm or the baby bunny he held at the petting zoo. Keep in mind that pets become members of your family, requiring almost as much attention and care as your children. Unless you and your child are ready to spend the time, energy, and money involved in feeding, walking, training, bathing, amusing, and loving a pet, consider buying your little one a stuffed animal instead. If your child has his heart set on a furry new pal, maybe he'd like a Build-A-Bear (www.buildabear.com) pet. Pet choices range from the traditional bear to dogs, cats, and bunnies, as well as dinosaurs and wild animals. In fact, purchasing one of their special "wild" animals, such as a cheetah or a panda bear, benefits the conservation efforts of the World Wildlife Fund.

Feed 'Em The Good Stuff

Many conventional pet-food brands are made from the inedible waste from beef and poultry farms that is produced using "4-D" meat (in other words, the animals that are "Dead, Dying, Diseased, or Down (unable to stand)" when they are prepared for slaughter. How healthy would you be if you ate diseased food at every meal?

Natural and organic pet foods use higher quality meats that are raised humanely without added drugs or hormones. The foods are minimally processed and preserved with natural substances. Certified-organic pet foods must adhere to strict USDA standards that ban pesticides, hormones, antibiotics, and artificial or genetically engineered ingredients.

If protecting the health of your pet isn't enough to convince you to switch, just remember that no matter how closely you supervise, it is almost guaranteed that at least one of your children will wind up with that pet food in his mouth.

Keep It Green

The boom in green design and marketing means that you can now find all kinds of eco-friendly toys, bedding, and grooming products for your pet. You can also find pet beds and toys made from organic cotton or recycled PET bottles as well all-natural grooming supplies.

Recycle

No matter what brand or type of food you choose to buy for your pet, it is likely that it comes in some type of can, bottle, or bag that can be recycled. Contact your local recycling center if you have any questions about the resources that can be recycled in your area.

Do The Doo

Look for biodegradable poop bags to clean up doggie doo rather than plastic bags that will prevent any decomposition over the years. For cats, steer clear of traditional clumping clay litter that is made from strip-mined clay and infused with carcinogenic silica dust and sodium bentonite. These are harmful for the health of your cat as well as your children. There are several eco-friendly, non-toxic, biodegradable kitty litter options available for kitty to take care of business (See **Use Your Green** in this chapter).

Get The Kids Involved

- **Adopt A Shelter:** Animal-loving kids can show their love for pets by helping out at their local animal shelter. Talk to your local organization to learn how your child can help. Ideas include fundraising, creating informative fliers, designing a website, or collecting recycled newspaper to line animal cages.

- **Pet Sit:** If your child is begging you for a pet, try pet sitting for a friend or fostering a pet from your local shelter. If your child is not ready to handle the responsibility of waking up early to feed, water, walk, and care for her pet each day, hold off on getting her one of her own.

- **Make An Eco-Treat:** Give your feathered friends a nutritious treat while helping your child appreciate the wildlife in his own backyard. Generously coat a pinecone with peanut butter and roll in oatmeal or sunflower seeds. Tie a string that is 3 to 4 feet in length around the stem of your feeder and hang it from a nearby tree branch.

U$e Your Green

Pet Food: Cats and dogs can enjoy a feast of natural and organic ingredients in Newman's Own Organic Pet Food (**www.newmansownorganics.com**). If you want to go for the gold, try Castor & Pollux's Organix line of organic cat and dog foods (**www.castorpolluxpet.com**) or the dog food from Karma Organics (**www.karmaorganicpet.com**) that carries the "95% Certified Organic" label.

Kitty Litter: Conventional cat litter is non-biodegradable, dusted with chemicals and made from strip-mined clay. Here are some better choices: Swheat Scoop (www.swheatscoop.com) is a natural, biodegradable wheat litter. Most major retailers will also have several earth-friendly options available in-store. The best part about these eco-savvy options? Many of them can be flushed or composted (for non-food plants) clumps rather than tossing them. Your best bet will be to try a few different options until you find one that works for both you and kitty.

Doggie Bags: Why place biodegradable doggie doo in a plastic bag that will keep it locked up for hundreds (if not thousands) of years? Instead, use a biodegradable waste bag that can be thrown in the compost bin (for use on non-food plants) or collected at your curb with other biodegradable yard waste. EcoChoices (www.ecoanimal.com) makes reasonably priced bags that are 100% biodegradable and made from non-genetically modified corn.

Green Pet Supplies: Planet Dog (www.planetdog.com) is a great source for eco-friendly pet supplies such as hemp collars and toys made from recycled materials. Castor & Pollux (www.castorpolluxnet.com) makes a "Head To Tail" line of all-natural pet shampoos that contain ingredients such as aloe vera, shea butter, lavender, and peppermint oil. And after a yummy meal and a bath, your pet can take a relaxing snooze on a pet bed from World Wise (www.worldwise.com) that is made from recycled plastic bottles.

Resources

Petfinder
www.petfinder.com
To find an adoptable pet in your area

Pets 911
(480) 889-2640
www.pets911.com
To find your local animal shelter

The Humane Society of the United States
(202) 452-1100
www.hsus.org

Build-A-Bear
www.buildabear.com

Chapter 7:
Adding On? Green Remodeling

Need a new addition to accommodate your family's new addition? Or maybe you're just looking to update the look of your kitchen or bathroom. Thinking green while remodeling or adding on to your home can improve the air quality, energy efficiency, and comfort of your home while saving you a fortune on future energy, water, sewer, and maintenance bills. For example, you can improve the energy efficiency of your new room significantly by selecting the right windows.

It's also important to reduce the amount of volatile organic compounds, or VOCs, that are released into your home from the building supplies and materials used in construction. According to the Environmental Protection Agency, contractors that use products containing VOCs "expose themselves and others to very high pollutant levels, and elevated concentrations can persist in the air long after the activity is completed."[7] Green building techniques minimize the emission of VOCs and other pollutants so that you, your kids, and your contractor can all breathe a little easier.

Top 5 Ways To Make An Impact

1. **Start Green:** Don't wait until the construction has begun to start thinking green. Ask your designer or architect to incorporate green building into the design of the project to make the best use of energy efficiency, waste reduction, water conservation, and use of recycled materials.

2. **Minimize Disruption:** Heavy equipment and other vehicles compact the soil and destroy vegetation, so look for ways to minimize the disruption they cause. Limit machinery to areas that are or will be paved or built over.

3. **Salvage What You Have:** If you're remodeling your bathroom or kitchen, seek out ways to salvage the materials that you already have. Old floor tiles could be used as the backsplash behind your range or as part of a decorative counter top. Salvaging material saves you money on materials and keeps these resources out of the landfill.

4. **Banish Toxins:** Conventional building materials emit toxins that are dangerously toxic to the environment and your family. Keep these toxins out of the air by avoiding formaldehyde-based adhesives, as well as toxin-emitting paints, carpeting, and finishes. Breathe easier by replacing these with solvent-free adhesives, water-based wood finishes, and low-VOC paints and carpets.

5. **Reuse and Recycle Construction Waste:** After your new room is finished, keep extra materials out of the landfill by making sure they are reused or recycled. In many cases, your contractor will be happy to take the materials off your hands for use on a future project. If not, post an ad on Freecycle (www.freecycle.org) or contact your local recycling facility or builder's exchange to ensure that extra materials are put to good use.

Green Tips

Get A Pro To Handle Hazardous Materials

If your existing building contains hazardous materials such as asbestos-siding, lead-based paint, or mold, hire a professional to handle the abatement. Hazardous materials professionals have the skills and equipment necessary to remove these materials while minimizing the release of dangerous toxins into the environment. It's safer for you, for your family, and for the environment.

Get Paid to Go Green

You may be able to earn rebates or credits by incorporating green designs or products into your home. Check with your local energy supplier to see if they offer rebates for ENERGY STAR appliances and other energy efficiency devices that you install. Call your local water utility to see if they provide free leak detection services, free shower and faucet aerators, free water audits, or rebates on water-saving toilets, dishwashers and clothes washers. Or check the Database of State Incentives For Renewables and Efficiency (www.dsireusa.org) for energy efficiency incentives in your state.

CHOOSE GREEN BUILDING SUPPLIES

Maximize your green design with green building materials that are better for your planet and your family.

Flooring and Finishes

Wood: Adding hardwood floors or cabinets to a room? Use reclaimed or Forest Stewardship Council (FSC) certified wood to minimize your impact on old-growth forests. FSC-certified wood comes from forests

that have been managed sustainably to protect the forest, the availability of wood resources and the local economy. Reclaimed wood is
high-quality wood that has been salvaged from other demolished or
renovated buildings. You or your contractor can find reclaimed wood at
building material exchange stores or via online sources such as Craigslist
(www.craigslist.org) or Freecycle (www.freecycle.org). Reclaimed wood
reduces the use of virgin materials, eases the burden on landfills, and
often costs less than new materials.

"Rapidly" Renewable Flooring: The swell of eco-design has brought with it
a number of renewable flooring options such as bamboo, cork, and natural
linoleum. These options are considered "rapidly" renewable because they
come from plants that can be grown, harvested, and replanted quickly with
minimal disturbance to the environment. Bamboo is a fast-growing grass that
is as beautiful and durable as hardwood. Cork is harvested from the outer
bark of the cork oak tree. Cork can also be used as an underlayment or as a
wall covering to reduce noise between rooms. Natural linoleum is produced
from such materials as cork, wood flour, and linseed oil.

Low-Toxin Carpets: Conventional carpeting is often produced using a slew
of chemicals that off-gas into your home for months after installation. Your
best bet is to steer clear of carpets altogether or minimize their use by choosing area rugs in place of wall to wall carpeting. When you do purchase carpets and rugs, look for products that are labeled as emitting low or very-low
levels of toxins such as acetaldehyde, benzene, formaldehyde, naphthalene,
toluene, and vinyl acetate.

WINDOWS

Choosing the right window for your remodel can go a long way toward improving the comfort of your home and reducing your future energy costs. In addition, you may be eligible for tax credits or rebates from your local utilities by improving the energy efficiency of your windows. Here's what to look for:

The U-Factor: What's your U-factor? The U-factor is a measure of heat that is transferred in or out of your windows. In other words, the U-factor tells you how efficient your windows are at keeping heat in during the winter and out during the summer. The lower the U-factor, the more efficient your windows are, so look for models with a U-factor of 0.40 or less. This number can be found on the window's label or on the manufacturer's website.

SHGC: Another number you should look at when selecting a window is its SHGC coefficient (Solar Heat Gain Coefficient). This number lets you know how much solar radiation the window will allow into the room. The lower the number, the less heat your window will let in. If you live in a hot climate, look for windows with an SHGC of 0.40 or less to reduce solar heat and keep your house cooler. You can also alter existing windows to reduce their SHGC coefficient by applying a low-SHGC window film. You can apply the film yourself or hire a professional. In colder climates or those designed for passive solar heating, look for windows with a higher SHGC coefficient to warm the room with solar heat. As with the U-factor, check the window's label or the manufacturer's website to learn more.

Storm Windows: Storm windows are basically a second layer of windows that do wonders to improve the energy efficiency of your home. Consider installing storm windows to provide additional insulation and reduce heating and cooling costs.

FINISHES

Paint: Most interior paints contain volatile organic compounds (VOCs), a major class of indoor air pollution and outdoor smog. Look for paints labeled Low-VOC or Zero-VOC that look just like conventional paint without all the stinky toxins. A number of manufacturers have also developed recycled content latex paint and primers. By incorporating unused stock and recovered paint into the mix, these paints are often less expensive than "virgin" paints while reducing the use of new materials and keeping the old paints out of the waste stream. Milk paint is another eco-friendly option as it contains all-natural ingredients such as milk, protein, and lime and can be purchased in a wide range of colors.

Wood Finishes: Conventional wood finishes are petroleum-based products that off-gas into your home for months after they are applied. Look for Low-VOC finishes (350 grams per liter or less), such as water or plant-based oils that give the same smooth finish while reducing the emission of toxins.6

INSULATION AND WEATHERPROOFING

Improve the energy efficiency of your new room with insulation and weather-proofing materials. Look for products that use recycled content and contain a minimum amount of VOCs.

Weatherproofing: Apply caulk, foam, and weatherstripping to all cracks and seams where unwanted air might be able to leak in. Look for caulks and adhesives with VOC concentrations of 70 grams per liter or less.

Insulation: Standard insulation typically contains 25% to 30% recycled glass, which is great, but you can do even better by looking for products that contain 75% recycled content (from recycled glass and cotton). This reduces the use of new materials while keeping the old ones out of the landfill. Also, look for insulation that is certified as "low-emitting" that contains little to no toxins such as formaldehyde and VOCs.

STARTING FROM SCRATCH?

If you are exploring the ever-exciting and often-frustrating experience of building a new home, take a look at the array of green design options and products available. If you are not going to swing the hammer yourself, start by hiring a contractor who is thoroughly versed in the U.S. Green Building Council's LEED Green Building Rating System. LEED stands for Leadership in Energy and Environmental Design, and it is the national standard for certifying green buildings. Homes that are LEED certified utilize the most eco-savvy techniques and products in their design and construction, boosting the home's efficiency and resale value.

Even if you don't go for LEED certification, you can use their resources and ideas to give your new construction a green boost. Homes built following green building standards may even qualify for special "green" financing, called Energy Efficient Mortgages (EEMs). Check with your lender to see if you're eligible.

Greensourcing

Green Builders: Check out the U.S. Green Building Council (**www.usgbc.org**) for a list of qualified green builders in your area.

Green Homes: In the market for a new home? Look for eco-friendly features that will save you a bundle on future energy, water, and sewer bills. Print out the LEED checklist from the U.S. Building Council website (www.usgbc.org) and bring it along while you house hunt.

Get The Kids Involved

- **Habitat For Humanity:** Is your child a budding Bob The Builder? Help him learn more about building and gain a greater appreciation for the roof over his own head by getting involved in Habitat For Humanity (www.habitat.org). The group works in local communities to build affordable houses with people in need, and they offer opportunities for people aged 5 and up to get involved.

- **Build A Green Bird House:** Gather up some leftover building materials from your renovation and enlist your child's help in building a green house for your feathered friends.

How To Build A Green Bird House

You can help defray the effects of habitat loss for our feathered friends by building a nest box, more commonly known as a bird house. Some of the same green principals apply to the bird's house as to ours. Check out Cornell Lab of Ornithology's Birdhouse Network (www.birds.cornell.edu/birdhouse) for more information about the habitat and house size requirements for different bird species. The following plans can be used to build a green bird house for small songbirds. Adjust the measurements as necessary to accommodate larger birds.

Gather Supplies: Use the leftover FSC-certified or reclaimed wood, nails, hinges, and glue from your renovation project. If you need additional supplies, hit your local thrift store or builder's exchange rather than purchasing new materials. If your wood has a smooth and a rough side, place the rough side inward as you construct your box. If both sides are smooth, rough one side up with a saw or chisel to give talons a grip inside the box.

Measure And Cut: For the front and back, cut out 2 rectangles: 5½ inches wide by 7 inches long (front) and 5½ inches wide by 10 inches long (back). Next, cut out 2 trapezoids for the sides that measure about 5½ inches wide and 7 to 10 inches long on an angle. Drill a few ¼ inch vent holes near the top of the box on the side walls for ventilation. Cut a square 5½ inches wide by 4½ inches long for the floor. Make sure your floor has some ¼-inch to ⅜-inch drain holes in case water gets in the box. All that is left is the roof. Just like most homes for people, the roof needs to be sloped and overhanging to shield the house from the weather and to keep predators from sitting on the roof and reaching in to gather food (eggs and birds). Make the roof 5½ inches wide by 8–12 inches long, depending on how much overhang you want.

Stick It Together: Assemble the box with your leftover nails and screws. Let the front overlap the sides and drill or cut a 1½-inch hole, centered 2–3 inches from the top edge of the front of the box. Use screws to make one side removable to facilitate cleaning. Nail the roof to the top of your box. Don't worry if you have a few gaps here and there; it's just extra ventilation for the birds. Just be sure the nest area will be protected from rainwater.

Hang It Up: For best results, leave the birdhouse unpainted and hang in a nearby tree at least 5 to 10 feet from the ground. If you really want to paint it, be sure to use the Low-VOC paint from your renovation in a light shade to reflect heat.

Need More Help? Check out www.thegreenparent.com for detailed information and a video demonstration of this project.

U$e Your Green

Wood: Look for reclaimed wood from companies such as Trestlewood Reclaimed Timber (www.trestlewood.com) or Pioneer Millworks (www.pioneermillworks.com). For new wood purchases, make sure the wood carries FSC-certification. (See **Chapter 12: Green Shopping Tips** to check out the FSC label.)

Sustainable Flooring: Sustainable Flooring (www.sustainableflooring.com) is a good source for cork and bamboo flooring. The bamboo from Hawa (www.hawabamboo.com) contains almost no formaldehyde and uses water-based, solvent-free finishes. For natural linoleum, check out the leader in the field, Armstrong (www.armstrong.com).

Windows: There are thousands of window manufacturers and many offer great energy efficient designs. Look for windows with the ENERGY STAR label that have a U-factor and SHGC to match your room's energy needs.

Paints: Benjamin Moore (www.benjaminmoore.com), Glidden (www.glidden.com), and Safecoat (www.afmsafecoat.com) all make Zero and Low VOC products, with more companies adding on everyday. Check out GreenSeal (www.greenseal.org) for a detailed list of low or no VOC paints. You can also try one of the many beautiful shades of milk paint from

Old Fashioned Milk Paint (**www.milkpaint.com**).

Insulation: Johns Manville (**www.jm.com**) insulation contains the highest post-consumer recycled content of any product currently on the market (unlike other insulation products that reuse scraps from industrial processing). Many of their products are also formaldehyde-free.

Resources

Building Green
www.buildinggreen.com
Green building news and a directory of green building products

DSIRE
Database of State Incentives For Renewables and Efficiency
www.dsireusa.org
A state by state listing of grants and incentives for renewable and energy efficient technology

Efficient Windows Collaborative
(202) 530-2254
ewc@ase.org
www.efficientwindows.org

Green Home Guide
www.greenhomeguide.com
A very informative and independent source for green building product reviews from industry professionals

U.S. Green Building Council
(800) 795-1747
leedinfo@usgbc.org
www.usgbc.org

Chapter 8:

Green Your Ride

Despite recent advances, car manufacturers have been painfully slow to get with the green program. In 1987, the average fuel economy of cars and light trucks peaked at 22.1 miles per gallon; twenty years later (in 2006), the average fuel economy for passenger cars hit 21 mpg.[8] Not much in the way of technological advancement going on there.

But with gas prices continuing to soar, our addiction to oil is not just painful financially, it's also painful to the environment, polluting our air, water, and soils. Car manufacturers are finally getting the message that Americans want greener cars that save us money while we save the planet. But even if you don't yet have one of these eco-cars, you can make better decisions about what and how you drive to stretch your green. Here's how to green your ride.

Top 5 Ways To Make An Impact

1. **Don't Drive!** The best way to maximize your fuel economy is to leave the car at home in the first place. Take public transportation, walk, or bike whenever possible. Even if you only do it once in a while, you will save money, decrease the wear and tear on your car, and reduce pollution. You will also be sending an important message to your kids that there are other ways to get around besides driving.

2. **Carpool:** Pair up with a friend or a colleague (or two) and share rides to work, school, and even the grocery store. You'll save money at the pump and at the parking lot, and significantly cut back on polluting vehicle emissions.

3. **Be A Smooth Driver:** Drive smoothly to get the most out of your fuel economy. Avoid jackrabbit starts, aggressive driving, and hard breaking. Five minutes late for pickup? Resist the temptation to speed. Besides increasing your chances for a ticket, speeding increases gas consumption and can even increase exhaust emissions.

4. **Get A Tune Up:** A tune-up will keep your car operating at its maximum efficiency, emitting fewer pollutants and sucking down less fuel. Whether you do it yourself or go to a mechanic, be sure your car is checked for worn spark plugs, dragging brakes, and low transmission fluid. Replace your air filter as necessary and be sure your wheels are properly aligned and rotated.

5. **Inflate Your Tires:** Keep tires properly inflated to reduce wear and tear on the tread and save fuel over the long run. Check your owner's manual for the recommended inflation level (this number is also usually printed inside the door frame of your car).

Green Tips

Drive An Eco-Car

Consider making your next family car a clean one. The market for environ-mentally-friendly cars has exploded over the past few years, so there is now an eco-savvy option for every family. These cars release fewer emissions into the air and help you go further on each tank of gas. With gas prices at all-time highs, who couldn't use a few less trips to the gas pump? (See **Use Your Green** in this chapter.)

Plan Ahead

Planning ahead to combine trips when possible will save you time, money, and energy (yours!). A cold engine pollutes up to five times more than one that is warmed up. So combining several short trips into one can make a big difference for the planet.

Lighten Up

When you've got kids, the car becomes the rolling closet, housing everything from spare clothes to sports equipment to last week's science fair project. But that excess weight could be affecting your fuel economy. It takes about 100 extra pounds to reduce your fuel economy by 1%. So, if you just have a few extra soccer balls rolling around, don't sweat it. But if you are still carting around that play yard and stroller (especially if your kids are school-aged), it might be time to clean it out.

No American "Idles"

Newer cars do not have to be warmed up like older models, so there is no need to allow you car to idle in the driveway anymore. Turn off your ignition any time you will be stopped or parked for more than a few minutes. In the winter, use a reflective windshield shade to help reduce frost and save you elbow grease with the scraper.

Cruise

If your car has a cruise control feature, use it to maximize your fuel economy. At highway speeds, using cruise control can reduce your fuel consumption by as much as 7%.

Park It

When you park, protect your car from the elements and it won't have to work as hard to heat up or cool down. In the summer, park in the shade or use a reflective windshield shade to keep your car cool and reduce fuel evaporation. If you have access to a garage, use it to keep your car cool in the summer and warm in the winter.

Maintain Your Ride

Take care of your car and it will take care of you. Regular maintenance and tune-ups, changing the oil, and checking tire inflation extend the life of your car, reduce the incidence of break-downs, and improve gas mileage.

Change Your Oil

Changing your car's oil and oil filters is another good way to improve its fuel efficiency. If you do it yourself, be sure to recycle the oil properly and fill up your engine with clean recycled motor oil. Plug your zip code into the Earth 911 website (**www.cleanup.org**) to find a used motor oil drop-off location near you. If you take it in to a service station, make sure that they will do the same.

At The Pump

Avoid "topping-off" your gas tank when filling up at the pump. Overfilling your car by even a little bit can lead to pollution caused by gasoline spills. When possible, get fuel when the weather is cool to minimize evaporation and prevent gas fumes from heating up and creating ozone. And seek out gas stations that use pollution-reducing vapor-recovery nozzles (those thick, accordion-looking plastic devices covering the gas nozzle).

Clean Car Washing

According to the International Carwash Association, washing your car at home uses between 80 and 140 gallons of water, while a commercial car wash averages less than 45 gallons per car. Commercial car washes use high-pressure, low-flow nozzles to minimize water usage. Washing your car at home also sends a bucket load of soap suds, gasoline, and exhaust residue directly into storm drains and waterways. Carwashes, on the other hand, are required by law to drain their wastewater into sewer systems for treatment. Some even recycle their greywater to further reduce water consumption.

• •

Interview with Green Parent Alan Durning

Alan Durning is the author of over a dozen books including *How Much Is Enough? The Consumer Society and the Future of the Earth, This Place on Earth 2001: Guide To A Sustainable Northwest, This Place On Earth 2002: Measuring What Matters, The Car and the City,* and *The Year of Living Car-lessly.* He is a former senior researcher at the Worldwatch Institute in Washington D.C., a sought after keynote speaker, and a consultant on a number of advisory panels such as the Sustainable Washington Advisory

Panel, the Urban Sustainability Advisory Panel, the Washington Health Foundation's Policy Board, and the advisory board of the Center for a New American Dream (where he was a founding board member). He is also the Green Parent to three children, aged 13-20; the eldest of whom inadvertently launched the family's "Year of Living Car-lessly" by wrecking their one and only automobile. Instead of replacing the family ride, Alan and his family embarked upon a year long experiment to get their kids to school, soccer, and birthday parties without a car. I caught up with Alan eighteen months after the experiment began and he and his family were still living car-lessly. Here's what Alan Durning had to say about his car-free existence.

Q: *Did you take much grief from your kids over this experiment or were they happy to be involved in it from the start?*

A: We've taken some grief but not as much as I feared. We did bribe them with cell phones so whenever they started to give me a hard time I just asked if they were ready to give up their phones. We still arrange all of their transportation so they haven't been as inconvenienced as you might think. Sometimes they complain when we tell them they will have to bike or walk somewhere . . . especially my daughter. She doesn't like to bike because it messes up her hair.

Q: *Have your kids had to miss many activities?*

A: No, they haven't missed any that were clearly important to them. For some things they didn't care that much about they may have had to decide whether it was worth biking to get there and occasionally they made the decision to pass.

Q: *Do you feel that your kids understand what you are trying to do?*

A: I think it goes back and forth for them. The adolescent mind is not logically consistent. But they are happy to take credit for it sometimes. For instance when there is a discussion at school about climate change they are pleased to point out that their family doesn't have a car. But there are also plenty of times when they just think the whole thing is a pain. Teens in particular are so concerned with fitting in with their peers and all of their friends live in households with at least one car if not one car per driver. So they alternately embrace it and think it's silly.

Q: *You have already surpassed the experiment's one year mark and are still car-less. Is this a decision that you continue to reevaluate or are you permanently car-less?*

A: We're evaluating it constantly. We did it as an experiment, not as a vow. We've stayed car-less month-by-month (we didn't sign another one-year lease so to speak). In fact, in the last few months it has actually gotten harder to be car-less because our transportation needs are changing. Our kids will be in high school soon and we don't know if it will be easier because they will be more independent or if it will be harder because of all of the social and extracurricular things that we hope they will be involved in. I will make no predictions about where we'll be a year from now . . . car-less or car-full.

Q: *What were the best and worst moments of your experiment?*

A: The worst moment? It was a cold, rainy night and we had taken a bus across town. My youngest was very cold and hungry and the bus was very late. We had no food to give him and there wasn't any place nearby to get him something to eat. If we had had a car, I could have had him home, warmed up and fed in eight minutes. Instead, he was crying at the bus stop and I couldn't fix it. By the time we got off the bus (which was ten blocks from our house) we were beginning to think he had a fever. My wife took him into a shop where he could stay warm and I ran home and got our bike trailer and we put him in it with a lot of blankets and got him home and put him to bed. It turns out he was better in the morning. But the feeling of not being able to do my job and take care of my children was by far the worst. The good news is that those moments have been very rare for us.

Some of the best moments for me have been cycling with my kids. As I mentioned, my daughter doesn't particularly like biking. But the other day we had a great ride on our tandem bike. We biked nine miles and she had never gone nine miles before. She didn't want to do it at first, but she was having a great time and she came home proud and beaming. That was certainly one of the best moments.

Q: *Do you have any advice for other parents who may be considering a similar experiment?*

A: I probably have too much advice. The first thing is to go slow. It might be too much to go completely car-less at first whereas it may be possible to shed one car. You can save a lot of money by shedding a car. Even an old, run-down car that is completely paid off will still cost you about $400 a month. And if you like to drive new cars and turn them in every few years you're probably paying $600-$650 a month. The scale of money that's involved is very, very substantial. So what you might get out of this is thousands and thousands of dollars in a college fund. That might be more motivating to many parents then the environmental benefits.

Parents also need to understand that there will be a lot more planning. Basically you are substituting time spent driving for time spent planning. The downside is a loss of impulsiveness. The upside is that you tend to set priorities and do things that are more important. You tend to make more conscious choices about how you are going to spend your time and this is a big plus.

Greensourcing

Car Rentals: Need to rent a car? Several car rental companies, such as Hertz (www.hertz.com), Alamo (www.alamo.com), and EV Rentals (www.evrentals.com) now offer eco-cars as part of their lineup. If you're thinking about investing in a hybrid for your next car, use this opportunity to try one out.

Car Sharing: If you'd like to take public transportation to work, but would still like the occasional convenience of a car for picking up the kids or running errands at lunch, consider subscribing to a car sharing program such as Flexcar (www.flexcar.com) or Zipcar (www.zipcar.com). For a fairly nominal fee, you'll have access to a car whenever you need it while saving money on gas, insurance, and car maintenance. Both companies also offer a selection of hybrid vehicles to green your ride.

Get The Kids Involved

- **Help Her Make Her Own Car:** If you and/or your child are handy with tools, consider helping her convert your existing gasoline motor to electric or even building your own eco-friendly car from scratch. A standard diesel engine can run on a blend of vegetable oil and diesel, or it can be converted to run only on veggie. Check out *From The Fryer To The Fuel Tank,* by Joshua Tickell, to learn how. After you finish greening your ride, race it against other green models in the Eastern Electric Vehicle Club's "21st Century Automotive Challenge." Check out **www.eevc.info** to learn more.

- **See A Show:** Attend a cool eco-car show so that you and your child can see the latest eco-savvy models and learn more about the technology behind today's green rides. Check out **www.autoshows.com** to find a car show in your area or take a virtual tour.

- **Two-Wheeled Fun:** Get your child a bike and teach him to ride it. Not only will this start him down the path towards vehicular independence, it will free you up from some of your daily chauffeur duties.

U$e Your Green

Gasoline-Powered Eco-Cars: The majority of eco-cars on the road today are called partial zero-emissions vehicles (PZEVs) that run on gasoline but use advanced technology to improve gas mileage and reduce pollutants. Hybrid cars also use gasoline but minimize its consumption with electric power. Hybrid cars emit fewer pollutants and use less fuel than their traditional counterparts, but these models will also be more costly than their gas-guzzling cousins.

Flexible Fuel Vehicles: According to the U.S. Department of Energy (DOE), all gasoline vehicles are capable of operating on gasoline/ethanol blends with up to 10% ethanol. However, there are also millions of cars on the road today, known as Flexible Fuel Vehicles (FFVs), that can run on E85 (85% denatured ethanol and 15% gasoline), and you may even be driving one without knowing it. Current models of the Cadillac Escalade, Chevy Avalanche, Chevy Tahoe, Chevy Silverado, DaimlerChrysler Sebring, Dodge Stratus, Ford F-150, Ford Taurus, GMC Silverado, GMC Savana, GMC Yukon, Mercedes-Benz: C 320, Mercedes-Benz 240, and Mercury Sable are FFVs. Check your owners' manual or talk to your dealer if you think your car might be able to run on ethanol. Check the DOE website at **http://afdcmap2.nrel.gov/locator/** to find an ethanol fuel station near you.

Biodiesel: Biodiesel is another great eco-friendly option. Biodiesel is a combination of diesel and refined vegetable oil. It burns cleaner than straight diesel and produces fewer emissions. Biodiesel fuel can now be purchased in almost every state in the country. The National Biodiesel Board maintains a list of biodiesel retail locations (**http://www.biodiesel.org/buyingbiodiesel/ retailfuelingsites/default.shtm**).

Or, if you'd like to run on straight vegetable oil, check out Golden Fuel Systems (**www.goldenfuelsystems.com**) or Greasecar (**www.greasecar.com**) to purchase a DIY conversion kit. Green Parents Woody Harrelson and Julia Roberts are active supporters of biodiesel, as are celebrity environmentalists such as Daryl Hannah, Willy Nelson, and Jack Johnson.

Auto Clubs: Sure, you could join any old automobile club to protect your family in the event of a roadside emergency. Or, for the same money, you could join a club like Better World Club (**http://betterworldclub.com**), where membership includes all of the standard auto club privileges as well as eco-travel assistance, discounts on hybrid cars, and bicycle roadside assistance. The company also donates a portion of their annual revenues toward environmental cleanup and advocacy.

Resources

Alternative Fuels Data Center
   U.S. Department of Energy
   http://www.eere.energy.gov/afdc/

Biodiesel America
   (310) 496-3292
   http://biodieselamerica.org
   In-depth information on bio-diesel from Josh Tickell

Grassolean
   www.grassolean.com

Green Car Congress
   www.greencarcongress.com

GreenerCars.org
   American Council for an Energy-Efficient Economy
   (202) 429-8873
   info@aceee.org
   www.greenercars.org

HybridCars
   www.hybridcars.com

National Biodiesel Board
(800) 841-5849
info@biodiesel.org
www.biodiesel.org

Fuel Economy Information
www.fueleconomy.gov

U.S. Environmental Protection Agency
Green Vehicle Guide
National Vehicle and Fuel Emissions Laboratory
(734) 214-4200
greenvehicles@epamail.epa.gov
www.epa.gov/greenvehicles

Veggie Van
www.veggievan.org
Josh Tickell's Biodiesel Journal

Chapter 9:

The Little Green Schoolhouse

Across the country, K-12 schools accommodate roughly 54 million students. Throughout the school day, these schools chew up piles of resources and create mounds of waste. According to the California-based Green Schools Initiative, K-12 schools account for 7% of all energy used by commercial buildings in the United States.

In the past, American schools focused only on test scores, with environmental initiatives barely making a blip on the radar. But today, many school officials are realizing that environmental efficiency saves money and the planet. In addition, green school projects such as planting gardens, reducing cafeteria waste, and using eco-friendly cleaning products provide a healthier learning environment which improves student morale (and boosts those test scores). And a greener environment at school backs up the eco-messages you're sending your children at home. Follow these tips to boost the green at your child's school.

Top 5 Ways To Make An Impact

1. **Save Money On School Supplies:** Before you head to the store to buy new pencils, notepads, and binders for a new year of school, check to see what's hiding in your closet from last year. A binder filled with recycled paper can be customized year after year to suit your child's interests (just redecorate the cover with stickers, fabric, or markers.) And you probably already have enough pens and pencils lying around the house to fill up a pencil case.

2. **Aim For A Waste-Free Lunch:** If you child brings her lunch to school, make it waste-free by using reusable containers to hold her meal. Skip juice boxes and let her pick out a cool thermos or reusable bottle to bring instead. Pack it all in a reusable tote or lunchbox. (See **"How to Make a Waste-Free Lunch"** in Chapter 3 for more ideas.)

3. **Ban The Junk:** Sodas and vending machine fare are not only terrible for your child's health, they also create waste and use ingredients that can be harmful to the environment. Talk with your school officials and other parents about banning soda, candy, junk food, and fast food from school grounds. Grants may be available to help your school initiate a Farm to School (www.farmtoschool.org) program that benefits local farmers while providing fresh fruits and vegetables at school.

4. **Prevent Idling:** A recent Yale University study found that children who ride a school bus are exposed to up to fifteen times more particulate pollution than average.[9] That's bad news for the 24 million American children who ride a school bus each day. Researchers estimate that this increased exposure is due to the idling and queuing of school buses. In other words,

as school buses line up and wait in front of your child's school, they are filling up with harmful particulate pollution that will stay with him throughout his ride. Make sure your school has a policy in place to ban bus idling.

5. **Go Paperless:** Encourage your school teachers and officials to go paperless whenever possible at school. School announcements and meeting minutes could be distributed via email. Daily lunch menus could be printed on a chalk or dry erase board. And classroom assignments could be turned in via email or on a reusable disk.

Green Tips

GREENING YOUR SCHOOL

Reduce Cafeteria Waste

Ask your school to reduce the amount of cafeteria food wasted each day by making a simple change in the way lunch is served. When the North Plaines School in Portland, Oregon implemented an "Offer vs. Serve" policy that allowed students to choose what they wanted on their plate, they reduced food waste by 47% per day.[10] Healthy à la carte selections, such as fresh fruit and salad bars, give students more access to wholesome foods while minimizing waste. After all, it doesn't do any good to fill a child's plate with green beans if they are just going to wind up in the trash.

Clean Up Your School

Illinois and New York now mandate that only environmentally friendly, nontoxic cleaning agents may be used in public schools. If you live in any of the other 48 states, find out what policies your school has in place regarding cleaning. If they still rely on an armload of toxins to do the job, convince them to make the switch. Order the free guide from the Healthy Schools Campaign called "Green Clean Schools" at **http://www.healthyschoolscampaign. org/campaign/green_clean_schools/** and hand it over to your school administrator.

GREEN FUNDRAISING

School fundraisers are the bane of many parent's existence. No sooner does the school year begin then the forms and catalogs find their way home: almost always for low-quality foods, junk, or paper products that you neither need nor want. So how can families raise money for their school without trashing the planet? Here are some great ideas for greening your next school fundraiser:

Sell Green Stuff:

Greenraising (**www.greenraising.com***)* and Lets Go Green (**www.letsgogreen. biz***)* are just two in the latest string of organizations that offer eco-friendly fundraising opportunities. Both have a range of products to choose from such as SIGG water bottles, eco-friendly cleaning products, and recycled office supplies that can help you spread an eco-friendly message while supporting your school. Another great green option is to sell reusable grocery bags through companies such as Chico Bag (**www.chicobag.com***)* or ReuseThisBag.com (**www.reusethisbag.com***)*. Imprint your school or club's logo on these eco-friendly bags to show-off your school spirit.

Host A Green Event:

Try hosting a zero-waste spaghetti dinner or pancake breakfast to raise money for your school. Hold the event in your school's cafeteria or your local fire hall and look to local businesses to donate food, reusable napkins, and compostable dishes, to make it a fun, community-building, eco-friendly event.

Pledge To Be Green:

Kids don't necessarily have to sell anything to generate money for their school. Instead, they can organize a walk-a-thon or obstacle course and raise money through donations pledged for every lap walked or obstacle achieved. The kids get exercise, the school makes money, the planet stays green, and everyone has a blast!

GREENING THE CURRICULUM

Talk with your school officials about adding environmental issues to the year's curriculum. Environmental education is easily incorporated into science classes, but it can also be integrated into math lessons, reading assignments, physical fitness tasks, or creative art activities.

RAISING GREEN STUDENTS

Seek Out Green Supplies

If you still need a few items after you have raided the closet and desk drawers, look for school supplies that are made from recycled and non-toxic materials. Choose art supplies that are water or vegetable based. Invest in reusable products such as rechargeable batteries and refillable pens, pencils, and scotch tape. Seek out products that use the least amount of packaging. Better yet, save money and packaging by buying in bulk (go in with a friend if you won't use it all).

Borrow or Rent Sports Equipment and Instruments

If your child has a passion for the piccolo or a flair for football, it makes sense to invest in the equipment they need to play. But, if they like to dabble intermittently in various sports and instruments, consider borrowing or renting their gear. It will save you money and keep your closet from becoming a hobby graveyard.

Pass It On

At the end of the school year, sell extra school supplies and books to reduce the clutter in your home and maybe add a little green to your wallet. Sell textbooks through Craigslist (**www.craigslist.org**) or Ebay (**www.ebay.com**), or have a tag sale. Too much effort? Donate books and school supplies to your local library or thrift store.

Special Situations: Yikes! Head Lice

Nothing brings out the anti-environmentalist worse than an icky case of head lice. Many parents go to toxic extremes (gasoline, lice bombs, and pesticides) in an effort to rid themselves and their children of these pervasive critters. Fortunately, there are plenty of eco-friendly solutions. See **Use Your Green** in this chapter for a suggested commercial product, or make your anti-lice solution at home. The key is to make sure that you kill the lice as well as their eggs. Here's how to get rid of lice without dousing your child in chemicals:

1. Use a commercial anti-lice product, or combine a few ounces of castile soap and a few drops of tea tree oil in the palm of your hand.

2. Lather hair, kneading the mixture into the scalp.

3. Rinse and rewash, but this time do not rinse. Wrap hair with a towel and let sit for 30 minutes, then rinse.

4. Comb damp hair thoroughly with a nit-removing comb.

5. Wash hair one more time with your commercial or homemade anti-lice solution and rinse thoroughly.

   Once dry, do a thorough inspection for any missed nits.

6. Next, wash bedding and clothing in soap and hot water. Stuff pillows in the freezer overnight to kill lice and eggs.

Greensourcing

Green Childcare: If your child attends a daycare or after school childcare program, make sure her health and that of the environment is protected during her stay. Green daycare centers limit your child's exposure to toxins and pollutants commonly found in playground equipment, furniture, pesticides, art supplies, and toys. The non-profit Oregon Environmental Council (www.oeconline.org) maintains a database of Eco-Healthy Childcare Centers in Oregon and beyond. They also offer an Eco-Healthy Checklist (www.oeconline.org/families/checklist/view) that you can use to evaluate your local center.

Get The Kids Involved

- **Plant A Garden:** Research shows that children are more productive and have fewer behavioral problems if they have access to nature at school. Help your child green up his school by starting a small garden to help classmates learn about nutrition as well as the environment. It can be as small as one or two plants that you and your child take care of together, or a large garden that is cared for by several classrooms.

- **Go Art-Deco:** Give your child all of the markers, stencils, and water-based paints she needs to make her own reusable lunch sac from an old tote bag. Or she can get together with friends to design a cool earth-friendly motif and print them on tote bags to sell as a school fundraiser. Several companies, such Carrotseed (**www.carrotseed.net**) and The ChicoBag Company (**www.chicobag.com**) now offer programs where kids can sell reusable bags as fundraisers, raising money for their school or organization and helping the Earth at the same time.

- **Join The Green Team:** Encourage your child to join forces with other eco-savvy kids to form a Green Team that evaluates the school's environmental programs and brainstorms innovative ways to improve them. Green Team members can initiate a school recycling program, present environmental education workshops in other classrooms, or lobby the school board to replace existing light bulbs with energy-saving CFLs.

- **Walk To School:** October 8th is Walk To School Day. Organize a "Walk to School" event with your child. Check out Walk To School (**www.walktoschool.org**) for resources.

U$e Your Green

Lice Treatments: Lice R Gone (www.licergone.com) is a pesticide-free and environmentally friendly way to get rid of lice.

Waste-Free Lunch: There are many fun reusable containers that you can use to pack your kids' waste-free lunch. Try Wrap-n-Mat™ (**www.wrap-n-mat. com**), a reusable "sandwich bag" of sorts that doubles as a clean placemat. They're inexpensive and come in a fun variety of colors and designs.

Backpacks: If possible, update and reuse last year's backpack by adding or removing fabric patches or designs. If you do need a new one, consider an earth-friendly brand that uses recycled materials such as EarthPak (**www.earthpak.com**), backpacks that are made from recycled soda bottles, or a backpack made from 100% recycled tires from Green Earth Office Supply (**store.yahoo.com/greenearthofficesupply**).

Paper: Recycled paper is good, 100% post-consumer recycled paper is better, and 100% post-consumer recycled paper that is processed chlorine free (PCF) is the gold standard. Look for brands such as Dolphin Blue (**www.dolphinblue.com**) and New Leaf Everest (**www.newleafpaper.com**), or browse Treecycle's extensive selection of recycled papers (**www.treecycle.com**).

Pens, Pencils, and Art Supplies: Check out Green Earth Office Supply (**store.yahoo.com/greenearthofficesupply**) or Greenline Paper (**www.greenlinepaper.com**) for a selection of eco-friendly writing supplies such as biodegradable cornstarch pens, recycled lunch tray pencils, or soybean crayons.

Notebooks and Binders: Mead's recycled notebooks and day planners (www.mead.com) can be found at major retailers. For recycled binders, check out the selections from Sustainable Group (www.sustainablegroup.net), Green Earth Office Supply (store.yahoo.com/greenearthofficesupply), and Greenline Paper (www.greenlinepaper.com).

Resources

Green Schools Initiative
www.greenschools.net

Healthy Schools Campaign
Green Clean Schools
(800) HSC-1810
http://www.healthyschoolscampaign.org/campaign/
green_clean_schools

Natural Resource Defense Council
The Green Squad
www.nrdc.org/greensquad/default.htm

Oregon Department of Environmental Quality
Oregon Green Schools Tools
www.deq.state.or.us/wmc/solwaste/education/schtools.html

U.S. Environmental Protection Agency
Clean School Bus Program
(734) 214-4780
www.epa.gov/cleanschoolbus

Alliance to Save Energy
Green Schools Program
www.ase.org/greenschools/start.htm

Chapter 10:
Working Green

Not long ago, the environment and business were seen as opposing forces. But today, companies both large and small are beginning to see the environmental and economic benefits of adding green to their bottom line. Whether you have a home office, run your own company, or work for a corporation, incorporating green practices into your workplace can save money, boost employee morale, attract customers, and protect the environment. As a parent, running an eco-savvy office also teaches your children that green means business.

Top 5 Ways To Make An Impact

1. **Install CFLs:** Replace traditional light bulbs with cost-effective and energy-saving compact fluorescents.

2. **Jump Into A Carpool:** If you work from home, pat yourself on the back for protecting the environment by not driving to work. If you do need to commute, organize a carpool with a friend who works in the same company or nearby.

3. **Ban The Water Cooler:** Eliminate the waste production and energy consumption of traditional water coolers and fountains. Instead, install an inexpensive water filter on the kitchen tap and keep a pitcher of filtered tap water in the refrigerator so that employees have access to cold, fresh water.

4. **Go Paperless:** Save paper, storage, and postage costs by reducing paper use whenever possible. Encourage all employees to think twice before hitting the PRINT button. Use email to distribute internal memos or customer newsletters. Share and edit documents using a wiki program. Reuse envelopes to circulate internal documents. Develop an excellent website that makes catalogs obsolete.

5. **Recruit The Stars:** It's difficult to operate an office these days without the requisite supply of electronics such as fax machines, copiers, computers, and coffee machines. Reduce your energy bill by purchasing energy-efficient models that carry the ENERGY STAR label. Many ENERGY STAR machines, such as laser printers, copiers, and faxes, also have an automatic standby mode that saves energy when the machine is not actively in use.

Green Tips

LIGHTING

Lighting makes up $1/3$ of the office's total energy bill. Cut these costs by installing energy-efficient light bulbs as well as motion sensors in bathrooms, break rooms, and storage areas where lights are commonly left on. For signs that are illuminated at night, such as exit signs or exterior lights, consider using an ultra-efficient light bulb that uses LED (light emitting diode) or HPS (high pressure sodium) technology. You can also install a photocell in the circuit for these lights so that they come on when it is actually dark and turn off when it is light, rather than at a preset time.

HEATING AND COOLING

Forty percent of the typical office's energy bill goes towards heating and cooling costs. It's easy to cut these costs and save energy without sacrificing comfort. Adjust the thermostat by a few degrees and encourage employees to dress seasonally. There is no need for employees to wear sweaters in the summer or short-sleeves in the winter. Install a programmable thermostat to turn off heating and cooling systems when the office is not in use. This can also be used to improve comfort levels by adjusting the thermostat to turn on for a few minutes before employees and customers arrive.

OFFICE EQUIPMENT

In addition to looking for the ENERGY STAR label, look for a copy machine with a duplexing feature to save time, energy, and paper. If your office has a vending machine, consider installing an occupancy-based device (like a motion detector) that shuts the machine off when no one is in the room. And make sure the office coffee machine has an auto-off feature.

WASTE

Reducing waste is one of the easiest and most cost-effective ways for an office to go green. Encourage the use of email over paper for distributed memos and documents. Set a paper tray in a communal area for paper that is clean on one side and can be reused as scratch paper. Skip the cover sheet on faxes, and instead print the correspondence information directly on the first page of the document. Recycle toner and printer cartridges, aluminum, glass, all types of paper, cardboard, and telephone books. (Call 800-CLEANUP or click on **www.cleanup.org** to find a recycling center near you.) In the kitchen, encourage the use of reusable coffee mugs, dishes, and flatware instead of disposables.

WATER

You pay for wasted water not only on your water bill, but also on your energy and sewer bills. Keep a sharp eye out for leaking toilets and faucets, and report them immediately to reduce water waste. Install water-saving aerators on existing faucets to cut water consumption in half. In new buildings, install water-saving toilets and faucets. Reduce the temperature on your office water heater to 120 degrees or less to save money and improve safety.

TRANSPORTATION AND PARKING

Employers that subsidize public transportation for their employees can increase available parking, attract and retain employees, and apply for tax credits. Additional incentives, such as better parking places, secure bike parking, or a casual dress code, might encourage employees to carpool, walk, bike, or take public transportation to work. Check out the Commuter Choice Program (www.commuterchoice.com) for customizable office transportation solutions. If possible, consider offering flexible and compressed work hours to accommodate employee schedules and reduce transportation costs.

GREEN PURCHASING

Look for the recycling label on everything from copy paper to envelopes to pencils. For paper products, purchase products with a post-consumer recycled content of at least 30% (100% is the best). Buy products in bulk whenever possible to reduce costs and packaging. Remanufactured toner cartridges for copiers, printers, and fax machines save money and reduce waste. Skip disposables and select reusable pens, pencils, and staplers.

FRIENDLIER FURNISHINGS

Each year, United States businesses buy about 3 million desks, 16.5 million chairs, 4.5 million tables, and 11 million file cabinets, and experts estimate that they throw out about half this amount each year.[11] Consider purchasing recycled or refurbished office furniture whenever possible. When you do purchase new, look for products that are made using recycled materials, sustainably harvested wood, water-based adhesives, and non-toxic dyes.

LANDSCAPING

Native plants are more likely to thrive without excess attention from a costly landscaper. Patios and walkways are great places for employees to relax and congregate while reducing the size of energy-consuming lawns. See **Chapter 5: How Green Is Your Yard?** for more organic gardening tips that can save you time and money at the office.

BECOME A STAR

The EPA is recruiting businesses to become ENERGY STAR partners. It doesn't cost a cent to sign up, and you can use the ENERGY STAR program to promote your business and gain access to energy and money saving resources. See **Resources** for contact information.

EAT AN ECO-LUNCH

If you bring your lunch to work, make it waste-free by using reusable containers for food and drinks and carrying it all in a reusable tote. If you opt for take-out, ask the restaurant not to put any unnecessary utensils, napkins, or condiments in with your lunch. If your office has a cafeteria, make sure the leftover food is donated to a local charitable organization. If possible, ask that food scraps be composted to cut back on waste.

STARTING FROM SCRATCH

In the market for a new office space? You can incorporate green building ideas into your workspace to benefit the environment and save a bundle of money. Natural light, fresh air, and non-toxic paints, linoleum, and carpeting are just a few of the new green requirements for employers such as Goldman, Sachs & Co. and Harley-Davidson Inc. Some municipalities are even offering incentives, such as faster permit approvals and reduced fees, to encourage green growth. Whether your office is large or small, use these tips from the U.S. Green Building Council to green your office:

• Locate your office close to public transit.

• Provide for outdoor garden or meeting areas.

- Reduce storm water runoff by planting rooftop vegetation or diverting water for use in landscaping.

- Recycle "grey" water from sinks and showers for reuse in flushing toilets and landscaping.

- Utilize alternative energy from solar, wind, geothermal, or another renewable nonpolluting source.

- Use recycled or refurbished materials in construction and furnishings.

- Look for paints and finishes that do not emit toxic Volatile Organic Compounds (VOCs).

- Purchase furniture that does not use formaldehyde as a bonding agent.

- Install operable windows and skylights that allow light and fresh air to penetrate the building.

Greensourcing

Printing: Look for green printing shops that use 100% post-consumer waste recycled paper and soy-based inks for printing and graphics. Try The Greener Printer (www.greenerprinter.com).

Cleaners: Look for a cleaning agency that uses environmentally friendly non-toxic cleaning agents (See **Chapter 4: The Green Clean**). Green cleaners are better for the health of custodians, employees, customers, and the environment.

Eco-Coaching: If you want to green your business without getting mired in the details, contact an eco-coach to lead you through the process. Eco-Coach (www.eco-coach.com) offers green business audits, sustainability benchmarking, and LEED certification consultations.

Get Your Kids Involved

- **Eco-Careers:** Is your child interested in an environmental career? Research the options together at Environmental Career Opportunities (www.ecojobs.com) or the Environmental Careers Organization (www.eco.org).

- **Homemade Memo Pads:** If your child is old enough for scissors, enlist her help in making scratch paper memo pads from scrap paper. Use a pencil to divide the clean side of a sheet of paper into four equal pieces. Your child can cut these out and use them as templates to divide and cut the remaining sheets of paper. Once she has a nice little stack of papers, she can punch two holes in the top and tie the sheets together with yarn, ribbon, or an old twist tie.

- **Design Your Lunch Bag:** Give your child a basket of art supplies and an old tote bag that she can jazz up with a cool design. The bag will help you carry your waste-free lunch while displaying your child's artistic talent.

U$e Your Green

Office Supplies: See the previous chapter (**Chapter 9: The Little Green Schoolhouse**) for a list of green office products. As with school supplies, you will find the best green selection through online retailers such as Green Earth Office Supply (www.greenearthofficesupply.com) and Sustainable Group (www.sustainablegroup.net).

Office Furniture: As more and more companies are demanding a green workspace, the market for environmentally friendly office furniture is flourishing. Look for furniture made from recycled materials, sustainably harvested woods, and non-toxic adhesives, paints, and foams. Herman Miller (www.hermanmiller.com), a big name in the office furniture industry, uses recycled materials and sustainably harvested wood in the production of many of its pieces. Baltix (www.baltix.com) has a nice selection of green office furniture made from such components as recycled paper, recycled milk jugs, wheat straw, and sunflower hulls. Steelcase (www.steelcase.com), a company known for its steel office furniture, uses recycled content in many of its pieces. Knoll (www.knoll.com) now creates office chairs from recycled soda bottles. Guilford of Maine (www.guilfordofmaine.com), a major supplier of office furniture fabric, now offers a line of upholstery fabric made from recycled soda bottles.

Promotional Products: Make a better impression on your customers and the environment by resisting the temptation to hand out bags full of promotional junk. Look for useful promotional items that send a message about your company's environmental commitment. Safe Designs (www.safedesigns.com) offers an extensive collection of useful promotional products made from recycled materials.

Paper Savers: GreenPrint software (www.printgreener.com) reduces paper waste by highlighting and removing unnecessary pages in documents. The software also includes a PDF writer and a program that lets you track money and paper saved.

Resources

Businesses for Social Responsibility
(415) 537-0888
memberservices@bsr.org
www.bsr.org

Commuter Choice Program
(202) 393-3497
info@commuterchoice.com
www.commuterchoice.com

DSIRE
Database of State Incentives For Renewables and Efficiency
www.dsireusa.org
A state by state listing of grants and incentives for renewable and
energy-efficient technology

ENERGY STAR
(888) STAR-YES (1-888-782-7937)
Federal Tax Credits For Energy Efficiency
www.energystar.gov/taxcredits
Small Businesses Information
www.epa.gov/smallbiz

U.S. Department of Energy
Energy Efficiency and Renewable Energy Network
(800) 363-3732
www.eren.doe.gov/EE

U.S. Green Building Council
(800) 795-1747
info@usgbc.org
www.usgbc.org

Chapter 11:
Eco-Vacations

Ahh! The family vacation. A time to decompress, have fun, learn some-thing new, and maybe even get reunited with your loved ones. Family vacations in this country are as unique as the families themselves; some offer the peace and tranquility of wilderness camping while others bring the fun, action, and excitement of a major amusement park. But no matter what kind of vacation suits you and your family, it is likely to cause an impact on the environment. If the term eco-travel brings to mind 75-mile hikes in rugged terrain while eating nothing but granola and sleeping on bare ground, it's time for you to think again! You can green your vacation by simply reducing waste on your trip or making a few adjustments to your itinerary. Whether you are headed to your local state park or a luxury foreign resort, here's how you can go green and relax with a clear conscience.

Top 5 Ways To Make An Impact

1. **Go Local:** Chances are there are nearby attractions that you have not seen or visited in years. Instead of stressing out about travel, accommodations, and logistics, take a relaxed vacation at home. Visit the newest exhibits at the local art and children's museums, aquariums, zoos, or botanical gardens. Grab some adventure at your local rock climbing gym or see the wildlife at a nearby state park. Mark your calendar for special events like children's theater, art shows, food-and-music festivals, book readings, and more.

2. **Consider Traveling by Train:** Planes emit more carbon dioxide per traveler than any other means of transportation, followed by cars and trains. If you are traveling in the United States, consider taking a family-friendly train ride to your destination. You will reduce your family's contribution to greenhouse gas emissions and save yourself the torture of flying with children.

3. **Line Up Green Lodging:** Check out The Green Hotels Association (http://greenhotels.com) or Environmentally Friendly Hotels (www.environmentallyfriendlyhotels.com) to find an eco-savvy hotel, motel, or B&B at your destination.

4. **Minimize Waste:** Reuse your towels at the hotel to save energy and water. Turn off the television and lights, and adjust heat or air conditioning settings if you are going to be gone for the day. Pack a reusable drink bottle to refill with clean water. And pack your own toiletries rather than using the hotel's mini bottles.

5. **Buy Sustainable Souvenirs:** Why bother purchasing t-shits or tacky knick knacks that have been imported to your destination when you can buy locally produced souvenirs that offer a pleasing memory of your trip? Locally produced foods, crafts, art, or jewelry support the community and reduce the pollution and transportation costs associated with importing goods. Do not buy souvenirs made from endangered species, hardwoods, or ancient relics.

Green Tips

AT HOME

Save money on your electric bill by taking a few minutes to unplug appliances, computers, power strips, and televisions before you head out. Adjust your thermostat so that you are not heating or cooling an empty house (but be mindful to leave the house a comfortable temperature if pets are staying behind).

UNPLUG

Reconnect with your loved ones and with the environment on a family camping trip. Leave the iPod, TV, and laptop behind and head outside for a little adventure. Have a picnic, watch the wildlife, and chat with a ranger at your local campground. If you don't have a ton of camping gear, save money by borrowing or renting equipment until you are sure your family will try this more than once. Check out **www.rei.com/stores/rentals.html** for a directory of REI rental locations or look for a local outfitter to rent your gear and support local businesses.

GO DIGITAL

Invest in a digital camera to capture your vacation's highlights. If you take a lot of pictures, you will easily recoup the costs of the camera in film and processing fees. The latest camera models come equipped with rechargeable batteries, but if you have an older model, just be sure to load your camera with rechargeable batteries and you're good to go.

SUPPORT CONSERVATION

If you visit a natural area on your vacation, respect the environment by following designated trails, paying entrance fees, disposing of your trash properly, and not harassing the wildlife. Take only pictures and leave nothing but footprints.

GET CULTURAL

If you are traveling to another country, minimize your global impact by showing your respect for the local culture. Read up on the environmental, economic, and social issues of your destination. Learn a few words of the local language and be sure you understand and adhere to cultural norms.

Greensourcing

Eco-Tours: The Sierra Club (www.sierraclub.org/outings) offers a number of organized family eco-tours throughout the United States, from snorkeling in the Everglades to camping in Maine. For overseas destinations, check out Responsible Travel (www.responsibletravel.com), Intrepid Travel (www.intrepidtravel.com), and Ecoventura (www.ecoventura.com).

Volunteer Vacations: If you're looking for an unconventional family vacation this year, consider a volunteer excursion where you and your family exchange work for accommodations, food, and sometimes even travel expenses. The Sierra Club (**www.sierraclub.org/outings**) manages a number of family service trips such as building new trails near Aspen or preserving artifacts in Dinosaur National Monument. Families interested in learning more about organic farming could contact the World-Wide Opportunities on Organic Farms (**www.wwoofusa.org**) to check out organic farms around the world that welcome families in exchange for a few hours of work. I-to-i (**www.i-to-i.com**) offers family volunteer vacation opportunities and free fundraising advice to customers who register and put a down payment on their trip.

Conservation Camps: If you are considering sending your child to camp this summer, why not look into one that helps protect the environment? If your child is an avid bicyclist, she might enjoy a trip with the Student Hosteling Program (**www.bicycletrips.com**). They offer bicycle touring trips throughout the United States and Canada for teens of all ages. Groups are separated by age so that 7th-9th graders travel in one group and 10th–12th graders in another.

The Maine Conservation School (**www.meconservationschool.org**) offers a number of overnight and day camp opportunities for children ages 8-18 to learn more about the environment. For example, the "Junior Explorer" camp for ages 8-9 provides the standard summer camp fare of picnicking, boating, and swimming while introducing kids to the concept of environmental conservation. On the opposite end of the spectrum, the "Primitive Challenge" camp for ages 15-18 is a six-day survival course where campers slowly lose a portion of their gear each day until they are left with nothing but a knife and a piece of cord!

Another good choice is the Wolf Camp (www.wolfcamp.com) in the Pacific Northwest. They have over 20 different overnight camps and a number of day camp opportunities for children ages 6-17, as well as a family workshop and camp opportunities.

Get The Kids Involved

- **Make Him The Travel Agent:** Enlist your child's help in planning your trip. From choosing a destination to researching the most environmentally friendly hotel to finding nearby natural sites to visit, your older child can pour through information at the library or on the web to gain a wealth of knowledge about the trip (and save you hours in front of the computer).

- **Play Greentag:** Log on to a carbon offsetting website (See **Use Your Green** in this chapter) and help your child calculate the carbon emissions that will be generated during your trip and purchase "greentags" to offset them.

- **Make Some Eco-Change:** Turn an old plastic or glass jar into an "Eco-Bank" where you can collect spare change throughout the year. Give your child stickers, markers, and paint to decorate the jar and cut a slot in its lid. Place the jar in a prominent location in the house and encourage family members to deposit their spare change on a regular basis. Cash in the funds before your next trip and donate the money to a local conservation group or charity at your destination.

- **Savor The Memories:** When you get home, help your child make a digital slide show of your favorite holiday pictures to remember the trip throughout the year.

U$e Your Green

Carbon Offsets: If you really want to negate the carbon emissions of your vacation, consider purchasing carbon offsets (also known as greentags). The money you spend on carbon offsets will be used to plant trees or support a renewable energy project, thereby "offsetting" the carbon emissions generated during your travel. Check out Carbon Neutral (**www.carbonneutral.com**) or Green Tags USA (**www.greentagsusa.org**) to calculate carbon emissions and purchase greentags.

Guide Books: Purchasing a guidebook is a great way to learn more about the highlights of your destination. Lonely Planet (**www.lonelyplanet.com**), Rough Guides (**www.roughguides.com**), and Moon (**www.moon.com**) offer guidebooks that include a wealth of travel information as well as facts about the environmental, social, and political issues of your destination.

Maps: Check out Green Map (**www.greenmap.org**) for a map of your destination that includes all of the sites' environmental, social, cultural, and historic points of interest.

Water Bottles: Any reusable water bottle will work for your day to day needs. But when you're on the go, you can't beat the Platy bottles from Platypus (**www.platypushydration.com**). These bottles are tough enough to be frozen or boiled, yet pliable enough to roll up for easy storage.

Resources

The International Ecotourism Society
(202) 347-9203
info@ecotourism.org
www.ecotourism.org

Planeta
www.planeta.com
For practical ecotourism information

Rainforest Alliance
www.rainforest-alliance.org
Information on sustainable tourism

Chapter 12:

Green Shopping Tips

The marketplace for environmentally friendly goods has exploded in the past few years so that now there is an eco-savvy alternative for just about any purchase you need to make. Seeking out green goods reduces pollution, conserves resources, promotes fair treatment for workers, and sends a powerful message to businesses about the importance of environment.

But let's face it: most of us cannot afford to buy everything organic and recycled-content versions of everything we need. How do you decide which products will make a difference? According to Josh Dorfman, author of *The Lazy Environmentalist*, "You don't have to go completely green all at once. You can prioritize by focusing first on the most important areas." For parents, that means our kids. Here's how to tread lightly on the environment while you shop.

Top 5 Ways To Make An Impact

1. **Think Green:** Save your green by thinking green. Shop with the environment in mind and ask yourself if you really need each purchase. Can you get by without it? Is it possible to rent, borrow, or swap with a friend instead? Curb impulse buying to save money and protect the environment.

Remember, even an item you buy on sale is a 100% waste of money and resources if you don't really need it.

2. **Buy Local:** Locally produced foods help to minimize the pollution and depletion of resources that go along with transportation and packaging. Organic produce that is transported from another country creates enough pollution to negate its environmental benefit. Local farmers markets are not only a good place to find bargains, but also a great place to find fresh produce and other locally produced goods. If you have to choose between local and organic, go local. If you can get local products that are also organic, you've hit the jackpot.

3. **Buy In Bulk:** Save money and the planet by purchasing items in bulk whenever possible. Buying in bulk is cheaper than purchasing several smaller items and it will minimize the amount of packaging that you need to toss. Need two cans of soup? Buy the larger can. Are you feeding a pet? Buy the largest bag of food you can afford.

4. **B.Y.O.B.:** Consider bringing your own bag with you when you shop. According to the Food Marketing Institute, the average American makes 1.9 trips to the grocery store each week.[12] Stash 2 reusable tote bags in your car, purse, or diaper bag to use when you shop and you can slash the number of disposable bags you use by over 200 a year.

5. **Buy Recycled:** Look for items that contain recycled content rather than virgin materials. Recycled content is used in a myriad of eco-friendly products from pencils to notebooks, jackets to sneakers, and even dog beds. Purchasing these products reduces the consumption of new materials, reduces landfill waste, and supports the market for recycling.

Green Tips

Minimize Packaging

Whenever choosing between two products, opt for the item with the least packaging or with packaging that you can reuse around your house.

Avoid Non-Recyclable Packaging

Choose products in containers that are easily recyclable. For instance, if your local recycling center does not accept #5 plastic, try to avoid bringing any home.

Skip Disposables

Disposable products take a toll on the environment in the resources they use and the pollution and waste they create. And while they may seem inexpensive at first glance, their costs add up each time they must be replaced. According to the Earth 911 website, a family of four can save $1,000 each year buy buying reusable and long-lasting products. Here's how they break it down:

- Batteries: You'll go through a mountain of AAAs and 9Vs in toys, flashlights, baby monitors, and radios. Earth 911 estimated you can save $200 a year by using rechargeable batteries instead of disposables in one CD player that is used at least two hours a day.

- Diapers: Save $600 by using cloth diapers (with a diaper service) instead of disposables (See **The Great Diaper Debate** in Chapter 3 for more information).

- Camera: If you take a roll of pictures each month, you'll save $144 each year by investing in a reusable camera rather than a disposable (go digital and you'll save even more on film and processing).

- Kitchen Supplies: Save over $260 each year on paper towels and napkins by using reusable napkins, sponges, and cloth towels instead. Also, use washable plates, cups, and silverware in place of disposables at the office or on your next picnic.

Look For The Star

Look for the ENERGY STAR label on over fifty types of appliances, such as toasters, ceiling fans, battery chargers, and washing machines. The EPA estimates that the typical American household can save over $600 each year using ENERGY STAR appliances instead of less eco-efficient models.

Is It Green Or Green-Washed?

The demand for environmentally-friendly products is booming, and manufacturers have responded by advertising their green. But buyer beware; not all products are as eco-friendly as they look. Many products are actually just "greenwashed," meaning they are made to appear eco-friendly without actually being eco-friendly. Greenwashed products may contain labels such as biodegradable, cruelty-free, eco-safe, environmentally-friendly, environmentally-preferable, environmentally-safe, or non-toxic. These terms are generally meaningless as they are not legally defined or enforced. Want to make sure you are getting the real deal? Here's a quick list of the labels that should catch your eye. In each of the following chapters, look for the "CHECK YOUR LABELS" box to help you sort out the green from the greenwashed.

Label	Look For It On:
USDA Certified Organic	Food
Organic Label courtesy of USDA AMS	
Fair Trade Certified	Food, Clothing, Wood Products
Leaping Bunny	Cosmetics, Personal Care and Household Products
FSC Certified	Wood, Paper Products, and Furniture
ENERGY STAR	Appliances

Be A Label Lover

Want to know what all those labels really mean? Here's a quick and dirty guide to the green, the bad, and the ugly:

LOOK FOR THESE LABELS:

Cradle 2 Cradle: Cradle 2 Cradle certification analyzes the environmental impact of a product throughout its entire life cycle. Products that bear this label use environmentally safe materials, are designed for reuse, use energy- and water-efficient technology, and incorporate socially responsible strategies into their design. The certification is found on a wide range of products such as diapers (gDiapers), cleaning agents (Begley's Best) and surfboard wax (Wet Women Surf Wax).

Dolphin Safe: The Dolphin Protection Consumer Information Act in 1990 prohibits the use of fishing methods that are harmful to dolphins and other marine mammals. In popular tuna fishing grounds, the "dolphin-safe" claim is verified by the National Marine Fisheries Service. However, tuna caught outside of these waters can be labeled "dolphin-safe," even if it is not. The non-profit group called Earth Island Institute acts as an independent watch-dog by sending its representatives on surprise field visits to canneries and docks in order to inspect the premises and report violations to the feds. They also have onboard observers that are granted access to inspections at the discretion of the company.

ENERGY STAR: Products that bear the ENERGY STAR label use less energy and less water than comparable models. There are more than 50 different categories of products that are eligible for the ENERGY STAR label including battery chargers, dehumidifiers, ceiling fans, dishwashers, televisions, cord-less phones, computers, printers, and even windows and doors. Look for the star before making your next purchase (www.energystar.gov).

Fair Trade Certified: If you are concerned about the environmental and social implications of the products you purchase, then seek out the "Fair Trade" label on foods such as coffee, tea, chocolate, rice, sugar, and bananas. The Fair Trade Certification is an independently verified label that ensures that farmers in developing nations receive a fair price for their product. The program also prohibits forced child labor, supports sustainable agriculture, limits the use of harmful pesticides, and supports community building programs such as health care, credit plans, and training workshops.

FSC (Forest Stewardship Council) Certified: The Forest Stewardship Council is an international accrediting organization that has developed standards for certifying wood and wood products produced from sustainable forests. Wood certified under FSC standards is rated according to ten principles that take into account the environmental, social, and economic impacts of the timber industry. Look for the FSC label on wood, paper, and wood products such as furniture, cabinets, and windows.

Greenguard: The Greenguard Environmental Institute is an industry-independent, non-profit organization that oversees certification of low-emitting products for the indoor environment. Look for the Greenguard seal on building materials, furniture, household cleaning products, electronic equipment, and personal care products.

Green Seal: Green Seal is an independent organization that sets standards for certifying environmentally sound products. Green Seal standards take into account the environmental impacts of a product from manufacturing to use to disposal. Look for this label on paper, wood products, household cleaners, and personal care products.

Leaping Bunny: The Leaping Bunny logo can be found on products that adhere to "cruelty-free" standards developed by the Coalition for Consumer Information on Cosmetics, a coalition of animal protection groups. Companies that use this logo on their products sign a pledge not to conduct or commission animal testing of their products or product ingredients. Look for the Leaping Bunny on cosmetics, personal care products, and other household products.

Organic: In order for food items such as fruits, vegetables, meat, poultry, and dairy·products to bear the organic seal, they must be produced without the use of synthetic pesticides and fertilizers, antibiotics, genetic engineering, irradiation, and sewage sludge. Animals raised for organic meats must have access to the outdoors and must be fed 100% organic feed that does not contain animal byproducts or growth hormones. However, the USDA draws a distinction between chickens and other animals. So cows that are raised to produce organic beef or milk must have continuous access to the outdoors without confinement, whereas chickens are not guaranteed access and can be confined.

There are three different organic labels that you may see on the shelves:

100% Organic: Products bearing this label can only contain organically produced ingredients.

Organic: Products can use the "Organic" label if 95% of their ingredients are organically produced and the remaining 5% are non-organic ingredients that have been approved by the National Organic Program.

Made With Organic Ingredients: This label indicates that a product is made with at least 70% organic ingredients, at least three of which are listed on the back of the package. The remaining 30% of ingredients must be approved by the National Organic Program.

Processed Chlorine Free: Products that bear this label have been processed without the use of environmentally damaging chlorine, which produces dioxin as a by-product. Look for the PCF label on all paper products.

Rainforest Alliance Certified: Under their SmartWood program, the Rainforest Alliance grants FSC certification to forest products that are verified as originating from responsibly managed forests in accordance with FSC Principles and Criteria.

BEWARE! THESE LABELS CAN BE DECEIVING:

Biodegradable: A number of cleaning solutions, paper products, and personal care products claim to be biodegradable. According to the Federal Trade Commission (FTC), the biodegradable label should mean that a product will break down and decompose within a short time of disposal. However, neither the FTC nor any other organization currently can verify a product's claim. In addition, just because a product will break down quickly does not necessarily mean that it is good for the environment. For example, the now notorious chemical DDT is biodegradable, but it breaks down into components that are actually more harmful to the environment that the chemical in its original form.

Cruelty-Free: This label is a response to the animal testing boycotts of the 1990s. It can be found on cleaning solutions and personal hygiene products and is intended to imply that the product was not tested on animals. However, this term is not legally defined and there is no agency that verifies the claim. Look for the Leaping Bunny instead to back up this claim.

Free Range: The free range label, found on poultry, eggs, and beef, conjures up mental images of animals roaming through endless fields to graze and drinking from fresh, cool streams. Unfortunately, this couldn't be farther from the truth. For starters, the term is only defined for labeling poultry, not beef or eggs. So a "free range" label on eggs is completely meaningless. The U.S. Department of Agriculture (USDA) requires that poultry labeled free range must have access to the outdoors for "an undetermined period each day." Five minutes of open-air access is considered adequate to get a stamp of approval from the USDA. Incidentally, open air access just means the coop door is opened, not that the birds are actually outside.

Non Toxic: Under the Federal Hazardous Substances Act, The Consumer Product Safety Commission (CPSC) defines toxic substances as those that are directly responsible for an injury or illness to humans when they are inhaled, swallowed, or absorbed through the skin. Products must also be labeled as toxic if it can be shown that long-term exposure can cause chronic effects such as cancer or birth defects. However, the CPSC does not legally define the term "non-toxic," so this label is generally meaningless.

Recyclable: Products labeled "recyclable" can be collected, separated or recovered from the solid waste stream and used again in some form or another. But just because a product is labeled recyclable does not mean that you will actually find anywhere to recycle it. Contact your local recycling center to find out what products are accepted in your area.

Recycled: The Federal Trade Commission (FTC) has developed "guidelines" on how the "recycled" label should be used; however, they do not verify its authenticity. They also do not distinguish between pre-consumer and post-consumer waste. Post-consumer waste has already been used at least once and returned to the waste stream (i.e., yesterday's newspaper). You'll also want to look for the highest percentage post-consumer waste possible. Pre-consumer wastes, such as shavings from a paper mill, have never been used. If you want to know just how "recycled" a particular product is, you'll have to contact the manufacturer.

Interview with Green Parent Leslie Garrett

Like many parents, Leslie Garrett spends a lot of time at the store. She had never really considered herself as a consumer, but as the Green Parent to three children aged 5 to 10, Leslie was always out buying, whether it was new running shoes, a new ballet leotard, or whatever else her family happened to need. But Leslie was becoming increasingly uncomfortable with the products that were available to her, and with her own family's level of consumption. As a journalist and author, Leslie began writing the syndicated column "The Virtuous Consumer", and later published a book by the same name in an effort to help families learn how to make purchasing decisions that are better for the planet. Here's what Green Parent Leslie Garrett had to say about Christmas, allowances, and looking her children in the eye.

Q: *Why did you decide to write The Virtuous Consumer?*

A: Before I wrote the book, I never really thought of myself as a consumer. I just wasn't someone who shopped unless I needed something specific.

But with kids, someone always needs something. I'm always out buying. I became really uncomfortable with the level of consumption that is considered status quo for families.

Q: *Have you always considered yourself an environmentalist?*

A: I still have a hard time calling myself an environmentalist, because it always felt like an exclusive little club. In order to belong your parents had to belong to a hippy commune or at the very least you had to have grown up with an organic vegetable garden in your back yard. I wear polyester…how could I call myself an environmentalist? I actually came at this way of life much more from a social justice perspective than from an environmental perspective.

When I was about 8 years old, my mother took me to see the play, *Oliver*. After we left, I commented to my mother, "Well, people aren't poor like that now." My mother's response was to take me on a tour of the city and show me that some people's homes were the size of my playhouse. My eyes were opened and from that moment on I became this little fundraiser who was forever trying to raise money for some cause or another. I took the lessons my mother taught me really seriously.

When I became a parent and subsequently became a consumer, the whole notion of sweatshops and child labor became an issue for me. I was increasingly bothered by the fact that I didn't want to be complicit in that. So I decided to create this column telling people how to shop with a social conscience. And it's not a leap at all to go from having a social conscience to having an environmental conscience because companies who don't care about their workers generally also don't care about the environment. To me, it's all part and parcel of the same thing.

Q: *Did you come across any major surprises in your research?*

A: I can be very naive. I have always assumed that products, if they are on the market, have been tested by somebody. Somebody has made sure that they don't contain chemicals that are known to cause problems. That to me was the biggest shocker of all . . . the number of products, whether they are cleaning products or personal care products, that are not only untested, but that contain ingredients that are known to cause problems. Yet they are still on the market. I realized that I have to look out for myself because nobody is protecting me.

Q: *What do you think are the biggest changes that parents can make in terms of consumption in order to protect the environment?*

A: I am very conscious of the fact that I have written a book about consumption. But the strong subtext is that we have to consume much LESS. I know that is really hard with kids. The average American child gets 69 new toys every year. That's obscene isn't it? My husband and I only buy our children one present each at Christmas time. And frequently we buy one big present that is the gift from Santa for all three children. When I tell other parents about this, many of them look at me like I've lost my mind.

We live in this gift giving culture where you pretty much don't show up at someone's house without a gift. Even kids begin to have this expectation that when people come over they will bring a gift. I think this teaches kids a message that you can be made happy by stuff as opposed to experiences or being around people that you care about. So I think the number one thing parents can do for their kids is to consume less. I'm the first to admit that this is not easy.

Q: *How can parents teach their kids to be "Virtuous Consumers"?*

A: All of my children get an allowance but ¼ of their allowance goes into a charity bank. Then they get to decide together as a committee which charity it will go to. Usually it's either a children's hospital or something to do with animals. That's what speaks to them. Then they save the other money and when they start bugging me for something I suggest they use their own money to buy it. It's amazing how quickly they decide that they really don't want whatever it was.

Another thing a friend of mine once told me is that when kids want something new, if possible, take the item out of the box. Because kids frequently look at the box and see the picture of kids that look like they are having the time of their lives in a setting with many other things that don't even come with the product. My eldest daughter is still outraged by the fact that the kids on TV are getting paid to look like they are having fun.

Q: *Do you have any advice for parents who feel they don't have time to take care of the environment because they are too busy trying to take care of their kids?*

A: First and foremost, what people often don't understand is that you're doing this for your kids. I don't know of a parent that isn't trying to give their kids the best chance to succeed in life. But at the same time, we are going to be leaving them with an unbelievable mess. This is far more important then getting your kid to karate or piano lessons. At some point in the future, when my kids are just furious about the state of the world that they have inherited, I want to be able to look them in the eye and say to them, "I did what I could." And I want to be able to say it with absolute conviction.

Greensourcing

Green Shopping on the Web: Co-op America operates two websites to assist green shoppers. The National Green Pages (www.greenpages.org) provides a directory of green business throughout the country while Responsible Shopper (www.responsibleshopper.org) provides detailed information about the social and environmental impacts of major corporations.

Get The Kids Involved

- **Make A Local Green Guide:** Harness the skills of a budding shop-o-holic (and reign in her spending) by encouraging her to research and develop a local green buying guide. She can canvass local stores and businesses to find sources for green goods and then compile her research into an online community buying guide.

- **Click (And Buy) Different:** The website I Buy Different (**www.ibuydifferent.org**) is an excellent resource for teaching your child about the environmental, economic, and social pitfalls of consumerism. Surf the site together to help him learn how the products he buys (or begs you to buy) make an impact on the environment.

- **Give Back:** If your child decides to do without that video game or extra pair of jeans, let her donate the money she saved to a conservation group or charity of her choice. For example, donations to PAWS: Progressive Animal Welfare Society (**www.paws.org**) help to provide vaccines, food, and shelter to homeless animals. Or for a $10 donation to Trees For Life (**www.treesforlife.org**) the organization will plant 10 fruit trees in a developing nation to help protect the environment and offer a renewable source of food to people in need. In addition, your child will get a tree seed starter kit with instructions for growing and planting.

U$e Your Green

Green Goods: In the market for recycled-content paper or organic, fair-trade certified coffee? Green goods are popping up at retailers large and small all across the country. Online sources for green supplies include Gaiam (www.gaiam.com), The Green Home (www.greenhome.com), and The Green Store (www.greenstore.com).

Resources

The Coalition For Consumer Information On Cosmetics
(888) 546-CCIC
info@leapingbunny.org
www.leapingbunny.org
Info about the Leaping Bunny Label

Earth Island Institute
(415) 788-3666
www.earthisland.org
For more information about the campaign for Dolphin-Safe tuna

Forest Stewardship Council
(877) 372-5646
info@foreststewardship.org
www.fscus.org

MBDC
Cradle 2 Cradle Certification
(434) 295-1111
www.mbdc.com
info@mbdc.com

National Marine Fisheries Service
http://www.nmfs.noaa.gov/
Information about the Dolphin Protection Consumer Information Act

The Rainforest Alliance
(212) 677-1900
info@ra.org
www.rainforest-alliance.org
Information about the SmartWood Program

Responsible Shopper
www.coopamerica.org/programs/rs
Research a company's environmental and social impacts before you make your next purchase.

The Consumer's Union Guide To Environmental Labels
www.greenerchoices.org/ecolabels
A comprehensive guide to environmental labeling on food, personal care products, household cleaners, and paper products

TransFair USA (TFUSA)
(510) 663-5260
transfair@transfairusa.org
www.transfairusa.org
Information about Fair-Trade Certification

United States Department of Agriculture (USDA)
National Organic Program
(202) 720-5115
nopwebmaster@usda.gov
www.ams.usda.gov/nop

U.S. Environmental Protection Agency
ENERGY STAR Program
(888) STAR-YES
www.energystar.gov

Chapter 13:
Food: Eating Your Greens

Your mother always told you to eat your greens. That advice is as true today as it was when you were young. But these days, green foods go beyond spinach and broccoli to organic selections of coffee, fruits, veggies, and burgers.

Conventional farmers use around 300 different pesticides to grow foods that are sold in supermarkets every day.[13] These chemicals pollute the soils and waterways, harming fish, birds, and other wildlife. Pesticides are also dangerous for the farmers who are exposed to them on a daily basis. The Environmental Protection Agency (EPA) estimates that pesticides are responsible for 20,000-40,000 work-related poisonings each year in the United States.[14] At home, these pesticides hitch a ride to the dinner plate on our favorite foods.

Organic foods are better for the planet because they are produced without the use of any of these nasty chemicals or genetically modified ingredients. They are safer for the environment, safer for farm workers, and better for your family's health because they keep these unwanted toxins off your plate.

Shopping for organic foods is easier now than ever, as both large and small grocers are expanding their organic selections in response to the explosion of demand. Even in my small town, I can find everything from organic eggs to organic chocolate. Eating your greens never tasted so good!

Top 5 Ways To Make An Impact

1. **Buy Organic:** Purchase organic products whenever possible. Foods that are produced organically are better for the environment than those grown via conventional methods. Check out the **Green Tips** section of this chapter to find out the best products to buy organic.

2. **Buy The Farm:** Searching for wholesome, fresh, organic food at a fraction of the cost? Look no further than your local farmers' market, where you can find organic growers selling produce without the supermarket premiums. For listings of local farmers' markets, check out www.ams.usda.gov/farmersmarkets or www.localharvest.org.

3. **Hold The Beef:** The production of beef makes more of an impact on the environment than any other type of food. According to a report produced by the World Wildlife Fund, more pasture is used for cattle than all other domesticated animals and crops combined.[15] Cattle also eat an increasing proportion of grain produced from agriculture, are one of the most significant contributors to water pollution, and are a major source of greenhouse gas emissions. The average American eats roughly 4 servings of beef each week. Skip the beef in just one meal and you can reduce the impact to the environment by 25%.

4. **Breastfeed:** If you have a baby on the way, consider breastfeeding her once she arrives. The health benefits to your baby are tremendous. According the U.S. Food and Drug Administration, breast-fed infants have lower rates of hospital admissions, ear infections, diarrhea, rashes, allergies, and other medical problems than bottle-fed babies.[16] Breastfeeding also helps new moms lose that post-partum weight. And breastfeeding is great for the environment, too: no waste, no resource consumption, no pollution, no problem.

5. **Compost The Leftovers:** Don't toss those bread crusts and apple skins, compost them instead. Composting will keep food scraps from filling up landfills and turn them into a usable product that's great for your soil. Check out **Chapter 5: How Green Is Your Yard?** for more information about composting.

Interview with Green Parent Jason Brown

As parents, we all want to feed our families great-tasting, nutrition-packed food at every meal. And as Green Parents, we'd also like to know that this food is as healthy for the environment as it is for our children. In today's fast-paced culture it can be difficult to meet those standards and still juggle the dozens of other things we do each day. As a Green Parent of five children and a Green Grandparent of three, Jason Brown knows how hard it is for parents to find wholesome food choices on the go. That's why he created Organic-To-Go (**www.organictogo.com**), a chain of fast-casual restaurants with locations in Washington and California that specialize in creating normal, delicious food that is also organic and all-natural. I caught up with Green Parent Jason Brown to get his take on the rapidly expanding organic food industry and what it means for the American family.

Q: For many folks, the term "organic" calls to mind unusual foods like tofu and couscous. Has the market for organic food expanded beyond this less-than-typical fare?

A: Organic has gone mainstream in a big way. You'll find organically grown produce from apples to zucchini at most neighborhood supermarkets, including warehouse stores like Costco. Traditional sources of organic groceries, such as Whole Foods, Wild Oats, Trader Joes and PCC offer a broader and deeper selection of products, but conventional grocers are all increasing their shelf-space of organic and natural food items.

Organic dairy; milk, cottage cheese and yogurt are some of the biggest sellers, why? It's because parents are concerned about antibiotics, growth hormones and other additives in these products that are a mainstay of children's diets. Organic baby foods are another booming growth item. Babies and children are much more vulnerable to pesticides because their brains, detoxification and immune systems are in a state of development.

Of course even food that may not be especially healthy can be made from organic ingredients. You can find a full array of snacks and desserts from chips to ice cream and pastries that have just as many calories or sugar (organic) as the conventional treats, but without the additives, preservatives, and trans-fats. Bottom line: you can get just about any and every kind of food you want in its organic counterpart. Remember, our grandparents and great grandparents ate essentially organic or at least natural foods. The volume of pesticides and additives introduced into our agriculture and animal husbandry did not take hold until between the first and second world wars. So when you remember that farm fresh, robust flavor of grandma's cooking, you are remembering what food tasted like when it was produced by nature without common and questionable additives used today.

Q: *Price is a real obstacle for many parents who might otherwise consider purchasing organic food. Do you think that organic food is accessible for families on a budget?*

A: Unfortunately there will be some price challenges, as the cost of organic food is not yet competitive with conventional food. Long term savings can be found with healthier eating habits, but practicality means making choices. Look for supermarket brand organic items and sales of course, and focus on buying organic items that have more risk factors when they are conventionally grown. Choose organic dairy and apples when possible and not necessarily highly processed organic foods.

Q: *What should parents look for when purchasing organic food?*

A: Buying organic is like buying anything else: look for freshness, quality and value. Understand that organic products have been produced to an exacting standard for quality and purity. Another great resource is the Organic Trade Association web site: http://www.ota.com/index.html. Check this site out to learn more, especially their special section on kids and babies called the "O'Mama Report," http://www.theorganicreport.com/ and check out the article: 10 Good Reasons to Go Organic to learn why it may be the right choice for your family: http://www.ota.com/organic_and_you/10reasons.html)

Green Tips

When To Buy Organic

Just a few years ago, the organic section in my small town grocery store was limited to tofu and a few herbs. Now, organic foods are all over the store, from coffee, to eggs, to salad dressing. You'll get the best health and environmental benefits when you purchase organic foods that would require the use of a lot of chemicals if they were grown conventionally. Foods such as apples, bell peppers, celery, cherries, imported grapes, lettuce, nectarines, peaches, peanut butter, pears, potatoes, red raspberries, spinach, and strawberries use and retain the most chemical pesticides.

If you have a baby, find room in your budget for organic baby food or better yet, make your own homemade baby food using organic ingredients. Babies have fragile, developing immune systems that cannot protect them from the adverse health affects associated with pesticides. Beef, poultry, and eggs are also good to buy organic, especially if you and your family eat them frequently. If money is no object, consider purchasing organic processed foods such as ketchup or soup. These foods may contain some, but not solely, organic ingredients.

If your budget is tight, don't worry about organic when it comes to onions, avocado, pineapples, mango, asparagus, kiwi, bananas, cabbage, broccoli, and eggplant as these fruits and veggies contain the least amount of pesticides.[17] And don't even bother with organic seafood as there are currently no standards in place to regulate their labels.

One final note: All grocers are legally required to place organic foods (especially fruits and vegetables) where they won't be exposed to the pesticide-laden water runoff from conventional produce. If your local store has forgotten that rule, remind them. If they still don't move the organic food, shop somewhere else.

Top 10 Foods To Buy Organic

1. Peaches
2. Apples
3. Baby Foods
4. Peanut Butter
5. Bell Peppers
6. Berries
7. Imported Grapes
8. Beef
9. Dairy Products
10. Eggs

Stay In Season

Thanks to the global marketplace, Americans have access to an almost unlimited variety of fruits and vegetables throughout the year. But it creates an enormous amount of pollution to ship this food thousands of miles from where it was grown to your location. Opt for local in-season foods whenever possible. Check out Sustainable Table (www.sustainabletable.org) for a state-by-state list of seasonal produce availability.

Go Veggie

A vegetarian diet is not only healthier for you, it is also better for the environment. Producing fruits and vegetables is exponentially easier on the environment than raising beef, pork, or poultry. I know it can be difficult enough to get your kids to eat veggies as a side dish. If you tell them their dinner is "vegetarian," you risk an all-out mutiny. But it's easier than you think to pull off a vegetarian meal. Think cheese pizza, mac and cheese, or spaghetti with tomato sauce to get you started.

Get Growing

Consider growing a few of your own fruits and veggies this year to teach your kids a little about the environment and remind them where their dinner actually comes from. No time for a big garden? Grow salad greens or herbs in a window box. Just about any veggie plant can be grown in a container, so even if you only have a small balcony or porch, you can still have some fresh seasonal veggies.

Save Dough

Don't get hit by organic sticker shock. Stretch your budget for organic foods by seeking out the deals. Purchase organic varieties of store brand foods. Sign up for the free shopper's-club savings card at your favorite store and search the web for printable coupons for your favorite items.

Support A CSA

Community-supported agriculture (CSA) is great way to get organic foods from a local source. CSAs usually require a seasonal subscription ranging from $300 to $500. But for this investment (which works out to about $10 to $15 per week), you'll get a weekly supply of fresh organic foods that often cost less than the same non-organic foods on your grocer's shelf. Click on Local Harvest (www.localharvest.org) to find a CSA in your area.

DIY Your Fast Food

Need dinner in a hurry? If you are lucky enough to live near an Organic To Go (www.organictogo.com), then you have plenty of access to fresh, organic prepared fast foods. The rest of us, however, can make our own fast meal at home instead. Toss together a PBJ with carrot sticks on the side or open a can of soup and a loaf of bread. Any meal you make at home will invariably be cheaper for your wallet and healthier for your family and the environment. Green Parent Bill McKibben, author of *Deep Economy,* put it this way: "Fast food is pretty much an environmental mess–cheap food grown under dubious conditions and trucked long distances that makes kids fat. But it's also a social mess–eaten fast, in noisy and anonymous buildings. A simple dinner prepared fast but with some love and care and shared together, even for a few minutes, around the table brings a family into focus."

Don't Bother With Free Range

The free range label, found on poultry, eggs, and beef, conjures up mental images of animals grazing in open fields and drinking from fresh, cool streams. But this is hardly the reality. For starters, the term is only legally defined for labeling poultry, not beef or eggs. So a "free range" label on eggs is meaningless. And unfortunately, it doesn't indicate much when it comes to poultry. The U.S. Department of Agriculture (USDA) requires that poultry labeled "free range" must have access to the outdoors for "an undetermined period each day." Opening a coop door for five minutes each day is considered adequate to get a "free-range" stamp of approval, regardless of whether the chickens saw the door and went outside.

Greensourcing

Green Restaurants: Eating out? You can still "eat your greens" by patronizing restaurants that use local and organic foods in their selections. Check with your favorite restaurant to find out if they incorporate healthier "green" foods into their recipes. Check out the Eat Well Guide (www.eatwellguide.com) for a list of restaurants that use local, sustainable ingredients. Try to minimize waste by using the minimum amount of paper napkins and plastic silverware and cups.

On The Web: If you can't find a local source for organic foods, purchase the conventional varieties to avoid the pollution and waste associated with transporting organics to your location. But if you really want to go organic, check out the following websites for delivery options: Diamond Organics (www.diamondorganics.com), Door To Door Organics (www.doortodoororganics.com), Fresh Direct (www.freshdirect.com)

in the New York City area, L.O.V.E organic delivery in Los Angeles (www.lovedelivery.com), Organic Direct in New York and New Jersey (www.organicdirect.com), and Pioneer Organics (**www.pioneerorganics.com**) in the Pacific Northwest.

If you are traveling, busy, or just not up for cooking, get your greens delivered from The Hungry Vegan (**www.hungry-vegan.com**). For a reasonable price, you can get a week's worth of healthy, organic, vegan meals delivered to your door (or to your hotel if you're on the road), saving you the hassle of shopping and cooking. (Makes a great gift for new parents!)

Green Grocers: If you are fortunate enough to live near one of the 200 Whole Food stores (www.wholefoodsmarket.com) across the United States, then you have access to a one-stop-shop for all of your green purchasing needs, from organic foods to green cleaning agents. Whole Foods has been criticized by focusing on organic to the exclusion of locally grown foods, a situation the grocer has attempted to remedy by listing the country of origin next to its produce. Also check out the green food selection at your local natural food store or co-op.

Get The Kids Involved

- **Make An Organic Smoothie:** Gather up your kids and your favorite organic treats to make a delicious and wholesome organic smoothie. Combine seasonal, organic fruits such as berries, peaches, or bananas with organic yogurt and milk. Blend and serve over ice.

- **Green Her Food:** Don't ban fast food unless you want a battle on your hands. Instead, arm your child with information about the health and environmental costs associated with the packaging and production of these foods. Ask her to research the fast food joints in your area to find out which one creates the least environmental impact. She can compare the nutritional information and environmental policies of all her favorite spots online. Compare the results and celebrate with lunch at the winning restaurant.

Check The Labels

Look for these labels when you shop for organic foods. See **Chapter 12: Green Shopping Tips** for label definitions.

U$e Your Green

"Meatless" Meats: If you're craving meat but trying to abstain, consider one of the myriad "meatless" meat selections in your grocer's freezer section. Boca (www.bocaburgers.com), Garden Burger (www.gardenburger.com), Yves Veggie Cuisine (www.yvesveggie.com), and Morningstar Farm (www.seeveggiesdifferently.com) offer yummy meatless entrees such as burgers, hot dogs, lunch meats, pot pies, and breakfast sausage.

Resources

Local Harvest
(831) 475-8150
www.localharvest.org

Sustainable Table
(212) 991-1930
info@sustainabletable.org
www.sustainabletable.org

United States Department of Agriculture (USDA)
National Organic Program
(202) 720-5115
nopwebmaster@usda.gov
www.ams.usda.gov/nop

Chapter 14:
Clothes: Wear Your Green On Your Sleeve

Most of us don't think twice about the environment when we are eyeing that cute skirt or baby outfit. But the truth is that the clothing we wear comes at a heavy cost to the environment. One-quarter of all the pesticides used throughout the entire world are used in the production of cotton. Not soybeans, or rice, or wheat, or potatoes, but cotton. In addition, most conventionally produced clothing is made using dyes and finishes that are loaded with chemicals. And to keep clothes cheap, many items are produced using child labor forces in deplorable sweatshop conditions.

The good news is that sustainable clothing and green eco-fashion have hit the mainstream. Gone are the days of scratchy burlap pullovers and horrid potato sack looking dresses. Eco-fashion now comes in every style, fabric, color, and price range you can imagine. It is entirely feasible to find beautiful, comfortable clothes that are free of chemicals and produced by workers who have earned a far wage. So whether you buy your duds at your local mass retailer or on the catwalk, here are some easy tips for going green.

Top 5 Ways To Make An Impact

1. Fix It: In order to get the most green from your wardrobe and your wallet, consider fixing or re-tailoring the clothes you already own. Learn how to sew a button or stitch a hem (or make friends with someone who can) to increase the lifespan of your family's clothing. Too boring? Consider giving new life to old clothes by re-tailoring worn out duds. For a fraction of the cost of new, you can turn worn out pants into shorts or a pre-pregnancy dress into a shirt or skirt.

2. Consider "Preloved": Hand-me-downs are always welcome in my house, where my little girls run through clothing so fast that I typically don't even bother making space for it in their dressers. "Pre-loved" duds save money and reduce the use of new materials while keeping the old items out of the landfill.

3. Seek Out Organics: When you have to buy new, look for organic fabrics that minimize the environmental impact of the garment's production. Fabrics that bear the organic label have not been subjected to synthetic chemicals for at least three years, nor have they been produced using any genetically modified crops. Cotton, linen, wool, and hemp can all be grown organically and used to produce green clothing.

4. Keep It Fair: The next time you are tempted to purchase a cheap $5 t-shirt, keep in mind the environmental and social costs required to make this garment so inexpensive. It's hard to feel good about buying a $5 shirt for your child knowing that another child worked in a sweatshop to make it. Look for clothing that has been independently verified as "sweat-free."

5. **Give Them A Second Life:** Don't toss your clothes in the trash. When you can no longer use a garment, pass it on to a local charity or thrift store in your area. If it is simply too worn out, cut it up to make baby doll clothes, blankets, or cleaning rags.

Green Tips

Buy To Last

Skip cheap and poorly made clothes that will fall apart after the first washing. Instead, save the planet and protect your overall investment by purchasing clothes that are built to last. Look for sturdy stitching, strong fabrics, and a minimum number of appliqués.

Swap-O-Rama-Rama

Want to have a little fun while you get something for free? Check out a Swap-O-Rama-Rama (**www.swaporamarama.org**) event in your area where you bring a bag of your gently worn duds to exchange for another. The events also host sewing and fashion workshops so that you can learn to get the most from your wardrobe.

Rebuild Your Clothes

A number of clothing manufacturers are "greening" their clothing lines by rebuilding garments into new designs. Under Patagonia's Common Threads Garment Recycling Program (**www.patagonia.com/recycle**), customers can turn in their worn out duds to be transformed into next year's line of fleece and cotton tees.

Don't Get Taken To The Cleaners

Dry clean and kids? That's just a bad idea to begin with. Steer clear of any clothes that require dry cleaning, but if that is not possible, consider hand washing delicates or seek out a dry cleaner that uses "green" technology to reduce its toxic load. See **Chapter 4: The Green Clean** for green dry cleaner directories.

• •

Interview with Green Parent Michael Lackman

Tracing their roots back to America's hippy era, Green Parents Michael and Shellie Lackman have been living a simple, eco-conscious lifestyle for over 35 years. They are very proud to have raised a daughter who has grown into her own highly developed sense of social and environmental responsibility. Five years ago, the couple decided to turn their passion for the environment into a full-time vocation, founding Lotus Organics, a company that specializes in healthy and beautiful clothing for the whole family. Michael has become an industry expert on sustainable and organic clothing, chronicling his extensive research and advice on his Organic Clothing blog (http://organicclothing.blogs.com). Here's what this Green Parent Michael Lackman had to say about kids, clothes, and culture.

Q: *How has the sustainable clothing industry changed over the years?*

A: In the past few years, there has been a huge explosion of interest in organic, sustainable and environmentally friendly clothing. It's grown past the basic "bread and butter" items such as shirts, pajamas, and underwear to also include clothing that makes more of a fashion statement. The industry is really growing and changing very quickly.

Q: *From an environmental perspective, what do you think are the most important factors that parents should consider when purchasing clothes?*

A: Parents need to look for clothes that are good for the environment as well as good for the health of their children. All parents are concerned about the health of their children, especially as we see the rapidly climbing rates of chemical sensitivities in both young and old. Your skin is a very absorbent organ and it can take in chemicals so parents need to be very careful. That's why they should look for clothes that are organic and not made with noxious chemicals. Parents should also be very leery of all "easy care" types of garments, especially for young children. These are products that make claims such as "wrinkle-resistant," "stain-resistant," or "mildew-resistant" that use formaldehyde and other toxic chemicals in their production. Those are the worst and the unhealthiest for children and the environment.

Q: *Do you think that right now, environmentally friendly clothing is accessible to the average American family?*

A: The problem is that if you look at sustainable, environmentally friendly, organic clothing, it will always be more expensive than something purchased at a large discounter chain. One of the reasons why clothes at these large chains are so cheap is that they come from suppliers and manufacturers that support sweatshops. Whenever you see a store that's offering t-shirts for $4, you can be sure that the conditions that those clothing items were made under were not supportive of the workers. Those workers were not paid a living wage. The good news is that the price of sustainable clothing has come down. And as the demand grows, you will find that even more. But they will never be as cheap as clothing that is made in sweatshops.

Q: *Did you ever have any problems convincing your own child to make environmentally friendly decisions?*

A: (Laughter) Every parent has problems with their kids, as you know! It's all a matter of compromise. You can't be rigid or dogmatic about it. There will always be some new style of shirt or some new type of jean, and your child will just *have* to have it, because everyone else has it. So you make sure that they understand the choices and what their alternatives might be and then if they still feel really strongly...well, sometimes you just have to be flexible. Choose your battles wisely!

Get The Kids Involved

- **Gather Up His Old Duds:** Enlist your child's help in gathering up his old clothes to pass on to a friend or a local thrift store. He'll see where his clothes go when they leave his dresser and realize that he is part of something bigger. WARNING: Don't try this with his favorite t-shirt or shoes!

- **Sponsor A Princess:** Encourage your daughter to donate her prom dress to a girl in need. Non-profit organizations like The Princess Project and The Glass Slipper have helped thousands of high school girls feel like Cinderella on prom night by providing free gowns, jewelry, and accessories.

- **It Isn't Fair!:** College aged kids who are concerned about fair trade and labor practices could join United Students Against Sweatshops (http://studentsagainstsweatshops.org) to protest unfair labor practices used to make university clothing.

Check The Labels

Look for these labels when you shop for eco-friendly clothing. See **Chapter 12: Green Shopping Tips** for label definitions.

100% Organic

U$e Your Green

Clothing: The list of companies getting into eco-fashion is growing every day, but Patagonia (**www.patagonia.com**) practically invented the idea. They said goodbye to conventionally produced cotton in 1996 and now only use organic cotton and other sustainable fibers. They also turn recycled soda bottles into fleece and created a garment recycling program that allows users to turn in their worn-out duds to be remade into new ones. Other eco-friendly clothing retailers include Lotus Organics (**www.lotusorganics.com**), Blue Canoe (**www.bluecanoe.com**), and Stewart + Brown (**www.stewartbrown.com**).

Shoes: Timberland (www.timberland.com) makes environmental commitments that go beyond a "greenwashed" label. A number of the company's global retail stores are carbon neutral, they use renewable energy at several of their facilities, and they provide a $3,000 incentive for employees that purchase hybrid cars. In addition, many of their most popular products now include a "Green Index" label that informs consumers about the chemicals and materials used and climate impact created to produce each item. Another company that is working towards providing us friendlier footprints is Simple Shoes (www.simpleshoes.com). They have great looking casual shoes for the whole family made from organic fibers, water-based glues, and recycled materials.

Resources

Sustainable Clothing Information:

Lotus Organics
www.lotusorganics.com
Offers in-depth information about sustainable clothing and organic fibers

Clothing Donations Sites:

Goodwill Industries International
www.goodwill.org

Soles 4 Souls
www.soles4souls.org
Collects gently used shoes for children and adults in need

The Glass Slipper Project
www.glassslipperproject.org
Collects and distributes prom dresses and accessories in the Chicago area

The Princess Project
www.princessproject.org
Collects and distributes prom dresses and accessories in the San Francisco Bay area

The Salvation Army
www.salvationarmyusa.org

Anti-Sweatshop Resources:

Co-op America
www.sweatshops.org

United Students Against Sweatshops
http://studentsagainstsweatshops.org

Chapter 15:
Furnishing Your Green Home

My house revolves around our living room sofa. It serves as a nap mat, play area, sick bed, trampoline, tea party table, snack catcher, reading lounge, and every now and again, as a place to sit. And while I thought long and hard about the color, price, size, and durability of my sofa before I purchased it, I have to admit that I did not think at all about its environmental impact...until now.

Conventionally produced furniture causes a shocking amount of chemical pollution, old-growth forest depletion, and waste. The glues, stains, and finishes used to make most items of furniture are chock full of the volatile organic compounds (VOCs) that "outgas" into your home. Children in particular (because of their developing immune systems) are especially susceptible to VOCs. The wood that is used to create furniture often comes from poorly-managed forests. Not to mention the fact that all of these large pieces of furniture need somewhere to go when they die.

Fortunately, eco-furniture is becoming as common as your average recliner, as most of the major furniture manufacturers are changing the way they design and produce their collections. Powder-based finishing coats, which not only are VOC-free, but require less energy and create less waste, can now be used in place of paint. Furniture giants, such as Hermann Miller and Knoll, are using FSC-certified sustainable wood and recycled content in some of their pieces. And furniture makers are looking past the showroom floor and designing furniture that can be easily disassembled for repair or recycling. That means that we, as consumers, won't have to give up function or style to go green. Here's what you need to know before making your next purchase:

Top 5 Ways To Make An Impact

1. Buy Vintage: The next time you are looking for new furniture, consider buying a vintage or "preloved" piece. Preloved furniture does not require the use of additional resources, and it lightens the load on landfills. In addition, furniture that has been around awhile has probably finished outgassing, keeping those nasty VOCs out of your home.

2. Buy It To Last: If you purchase an item that is flimsy to begin with, it probably won't last long in a house filled with kids. Invest in durable furniture that will save you money over the long run in replacement costs.

3. Look For The Label: If you are in the market for new wood furniture, make sure it bears the seal of approval from the Forest Stewardship Council (FSC). (See Check The Labels below) Furniture that is FSC-certified is produced from trees grown and harvested in a sustainable manner.

4. Go Low Toxic: Did you ever notice how a new piece of furniture stinks when you first bring it home? That stink is the gases seeping out of the furniture's glues, paints, and finishes, and it is loaded with chemicals that you really don't want to breathe, like VOCs and formaldehyde. Keep these toxins out of the air and out of your home by selecting furniture that uses water-based adhesives and natural treatments.

5. **Pass It On:** Don't send your furniture off to the landfill graveyard. Even if it is broken, you will likely find someone who will be glad to take it off of your hands (and even pay you for it) at a yard sale or at sites such as Craigslist (**www.craiglist.org**) or eBay (**www.ebay.com**). If that doesn't work, give it away for free at your local thrift store or on Freecycle (**www.freecycle.org**). Last resort: stick it in your front yard with a FREE sign on it.

Green Tips

Go Ape Over Bamboo

Bamboo is a fast-growing grass that has become the exciting new material in the eco-furniture industry. Designers are using it for everything from flooring to furniture to window blinds. It has the look and durability of hardwood, but renews much more rapidly, taking pressure off of hardwood forests. Most bamboo originates in China and is grown with few or no pesticides.

Recycled Materials

Look for furniture made from reclaimed wood and other recycled materials. Reclaimed wood is salvaged from old furniture or houses. Reusing this wood and other recycled material in furniture uses less energy and resources than virgin materials and provides a market for the recycling industry.

Can You Take It Apart?

Kids are rough on furniture, so look for pieces that are easy to repair, disassemble, and, if necessary, recycle. You will save money and get more life out of your furniture if it lends itself to an easy repair. Steer clear of large, inseparable pieces that are useless if broken.

• •

Interview with Green Parent Lori Helman

Green Parent Lori Helman knows how to juggle. She is a stay-at-home mom to four young children. She's their homeschool teacher, as well. And as if that weren't enough to keep her busy, Lori is also the founder of Momma's Baby (www.mommasbaby.com), an eco-friendly boutique that specializes in natural and organic products for moms and babies. I chatted with Lori to find out her secret to keeping four children safe, happy and healthy without wreaking havoc on the planet (or losing her sanity!)

Q: *Why did you open up Momma's Baby?*

A: I started my company after the birth of my first child, because I had a passion for finding healthy and sustainable products to care for my baby. I began by selling cloth diapers and then gradually expanded my business as I found eco-friendly and healthy products for babies and parents.

Q: *Where do you think parents should focus when making healthy and sustainable choices for their families?*

A: To me, there are two things that I consider to be the most important. The first is what your kids eat. It's so important to eat organic foods whenever possible, especially for babies. At home here, I offer foods that we as a family are eating such as organic peas, organic carrots etc. This makes it more economical for a family and healthy for the baby. I rarely ever purchase canned baby foods. But even if you can't feed them all organic, it's important to watch out and make sure that your kids are not getting a lot of chemicals, additives, and preservatives in their foods. I also believe in nursing babies, especially during that first year.

The second thing that parents should focus on is their children's bedding. Kids spend such a large amount of time laying down and sleeping, whether it's in a bed, or a basket, or a crib, and if their bedding is not organic or natural, they will breathe in all of the chemicals that are in their mattresses and bedding. So I think having an eco-friendly, healthy bed for the child to sleep on is very critical.

Q: *How do you make your kids part of your efforts to be eco-friendly?*

A: Children will always follow the parent's footsteps, because they look up to us. If we, as parents, aren't eating right and doing the right things, then our children aren't going to do it. So in our house, we don't get all kinds of junk food. And when we go to the store, the kids go shopping with me and they know what products to look for. From the time my kids are little, I talk about the importance of eating the right things. They know that mommas always concerned about what they sleep on and what they wear and that I like it to be natural and healthy for them. My little boy is eight and he already knows so much at his age, it's just incredible. I think that children will learn by example and hopefully their lifestyle will also reflect that as they grow older.

Lori's Organic Playdough Recipe:

While we spoke on the phone, this incredible mom's four young children were playing silently in the same room with some organic playdough that Lori had mixed up for the occasion. She was generous enough to share with us that magic recipe!

Lori's Organic Playdough

1 cup organic flour
1/2 cup sea salt
2 Tbs. cream of tartar
1 cup filtered water
1 Tbs. vegetable oil

Mix flour, salt and cream of tartar in a saucepan. Combine water and oil in a small bowl. Stir into flour mixture gradually. Cook over medium heat for 5 minutes or until very thick, stirring constantly. Remove and allow to cool for a few minutes. Knead until smooth. Store in an airtight container.

How To Green Your Nursery

When a new baby is on the way, it is easy to succumb to all of the adorable products and furnishings that are marketed as baby care "essentials." But what do you really need? And how do you choose products that are safe for your baby and for the environment? Here's how to green your baby's nursery.

1. **Don't Go Overboard:** Contrary to the marketing hype, you do not need all of the baby furniture that comes in most sets. Talk to your friends and family about which items they found most useful, and skip the rest.

2. **Buy Pieces That Grow With Him:** When selecting baby furniture, look for items that will grow with your child, such as cribs that convert to toddler beds or changing tables that become dressers. These items will save you a fortune in the long run and keep your old stuff from filling up the landfill.

3. **No-VOCs:** Babies, with their fragile and developing immune systems, are especially susceptible to the potential health risks associated with VOCs. Paint your nursery with low or no-VOC paint. Use low-VOC carpet (or better yet, save yourself the cleaning hassle and skip carpeting altogether).

4. **Buy A Green Crib:** If you can get a secondhand crib from a reliable source that meets all of today's safety requirements, you have hit the jackpot! You will save money and the environment. But if you do need to purchase a new crib, be very selective. Cheap furniture, while tempting for the budget, typically contains formaldehyde and high-VOC particle board. Steer clear of products that carry the label "known to the state of California to cause cancer or reproductive toxicity," as it likely contains these toxins. If your budget allows, look for a crib that uses FSC-certified wood.

Get The Kids Involved

- **Green Her Room:** Even if all your child does in her room is sleep, she will spend ⅓ of her growing years in her bedroom. Bump this number up even more if she hangs out in her room to read, play, or watch T.V. So it makes sense to make this room as green as possible, both for her health and for that of the environment. This is especially important for infants, so check out **How to Green Your Nursery** in Chapter 15 for ideas.

- **DIY Art Tables:** If your child loves art, free up your kitchen table by giving him a dedicated space for all of his coloring, painting, and play-doughing projects. Scour secondhand stores or yard sales for a small table and chair set that your child can decorate with paint, crayons, or stickers. Stock it with his favorite supplies, and he will be ready to create whenever the mood strikes.

Check The Labels

Look for these labels as you search for environmentally friendly furniture. See **Green Shopping Tips** in Chapter 12 for the definitions.

U$e Your Green

Furniture For Babies and Kids: Check out Lifekind (www.lifekind.com) and Sage Baby (www.sagebabynyc.com) for non-toxic cribs and organic baby bedding. Ikea (www.ikea.com) has a great selection of inexpensive and fun furniture for kids and adults.

Furniture For Everyone Else: Look for furniture that uses reclaimed wood, recycled content, and non-toxic finishes and adhesives. Green furniture manufacturers include Haworth (**www.haworth.com**), Herman Miller (**www.hermanmiller.com**), and Knoll (**www.knoll.com**). Also check out Eco Designz (**www.ecodesignz.com**), Greener Lifestyles (**www.greenerlifestyles.com**), and Viva Terra (**www.vivaterra.com**).

Resources

Forest Stewardship Council
www.fsc.org/en

Greenguard Environmental Institute
(800) 427-9681
info@greenguard.org
www.greenguard.org

Rainforest Alliance
SmartWood Program
(802) 434-5491
info@rao.org

U.S. Green Building Council
(800) 795-1747
leedinfo@usgbc.org
www.usgbc.org

Chapter 16:
Green Beauty

The bathroom is often regarded as a sanctuary of the family home: a place to unwind in a hot shower, pamper oneself with a spa treatment, or simply take care of business in relative privacy. Unfortunately, however, the average American bathroom has become a haven of chemical exposure, housing a variety of personal care products that may be harmful to your health.

Just how toxic is your bathroom? To date, 89% of the 10,500 ingredients used in personal care products have not been evaluated for safety by the FDA, the Cosmetic Ingredient Review (an in-house panel appointed by the cosmetics industry), or anyone else.[18] Of particular concern are ingredients such as phthalates, parabens, formaldehyde, and mercury that are showing up in a variety of personal care product formulas. Current scientific research shows that many of these ingredients present a serious risk to human and environmental health. FDA officials and health experts throughout the world are particularly concerned about the "cocktail effect" that may occur when different chemicals and toxins are mixed in the body and then subsequently in the environment.

A 2004 survey by the Environmental Working Group, a nonprofit research group, found that the average adult uses approximately nine personal care products each day, for a total of 126 unique chemical ingredients.[19] While some products are tested for reactions such as skin redness, rashes, or stinging, there is little to no information about the long-term safety of these chemical cocktails for either humans or the environment.

The good news is that you don't have to give up washing your hair or smelling good in order to protect your health and be nice to the planet. There are safe, non-toxic alternatives to virtually every personal care product your family needs. Here's how to look and feel clean and beautiful without indulging in the chemical cocktail.

Top 5 Ways To Make An Impact

1. **Read The Labels:** Take five seconds to read the label and put down any product that contains phthalates, mercury, toluene, lead, formaldehyde, petroleum distillates, parabens (hormone-disrupting preservatives such as methylparaben, butylparaben, ethylparaben, isobutylparaben, and propylparaben), or BHA. These chemicals are considered the most detrimental to human and environmental health.

2. **Use A Little Less:** Revaluate your beauty regimen to see if you can get by with a little less. Do you really need all of those beauty products in your cabinet? For each product you eliminate, you'll save money and reduce the chemicals in your body and in the environment.

3. **Be Kind To Animals:** Animal testing is unnecessary, unethical, and just plain cruel. Look for the "Leaping Bunny" label to make sure your beauty products are "cruelty-free." This symbol, created by the The

Coalition For Consumer Information On Cosmetics, is the only international standard for personal care products indicating that they have not been tested on animals.

4. **Don't Leave A Carbon Footprint On Your Face:** O.K., so you've cut back on the amount of oil and gas you use in your car, now how about reducing the carbon footprint of the chemicals you use on your body? Petroleum derivatives are found in a surprising number of personal care products such as lip balm, lotions, and lubricants, as well as the plastics used in sanitary products. Pass on products that use petroleum or its derivatives (paraffin oil, propylene glycol, and ethylene) and look for alternatives such as beeswax, cocoa butter, and vegetable oils instead.

5. **Skip Disposables:** According the environmental news website Grist (www.grist.org), two billion disposable razors end up in United States landfills each year.[20] Invest in a reusable and refillable razor to save money and take a knick out the waste stream.

Green Tips

Smell Clean, Skip Fragrance

Many products that are supposedly "fragrance-free" actually contain "fragrance" as an ingredient as well as additional masking fragrances that give the product a neutral odor. If you are looking for a fragrance-free product, scrutinize the label and make sure the term "fragrance" is not listed as an ingredient.

Be Mild To Dry Skin

If your skin is chronically dry, try using a milder soap that is gentler on your skin. Soap is made to remove dirt and grease from your skin, but harsh, abrasive soap may also remove too much of your skin's natural oils, creating the need for you to use an additional product. Look for a milder soap that can reduce dryness naturally.

DIY

Got some extra time and ambition on your hands? Consider making your own personal care products. Check out *Naturally Healthy Skin: Tips & Techniques for a Lifetime of Radiant Skin* by Stephanie Tourles, or click on My Beauty Recipes (**www.mybeautyrecipes.com**) for recipes for everything from shampoo to mouthwash.

Interview with Green Parent David Steinman

Twenty years ago, David Steinman was a young journalist working on a story for *LA Weekly*, when he learned that fish in the Santa Monica Bay were tainted with chemicals. He began to wonder how many poisons were in other foods he ate and began to research the levels of industrial pollutants and pesticides in human blood. Over the years, this Green Parent of two teenagers has continued to study and write about the safety of the chemicals that we are exposed to on a daily basis. His books include *Diet for a Poisoned Planet, The Safe Shopper's Bible,* and *Safe Trip to Eden: Ten Steps to Save the Planet Earth from Global Warming Meltdown.* Here's what Green Parent David Steinman had to say about the safety of your bath and beauty products.

Q: *What advice do you have for parents who are looking for safe and eco-friendly health and beauty products?*

A: My own testing revealed that almost every mainstream bath product is contaminated with undisclosed carcinogens, especially the ones with cartoon characters on the packaging. Skin lotion also tends to contain it. So I would definitely advise parents to avoid those products and look for safer alternatives. The products that we tested that were safe were Aubrey Organics and Dr. Bronner. Parents should also be very cautious about letting their children use facial makeup, play cosmetics, and dark hair dyes as these products tend to contain carcinogens.

Q: *What are the worst chemicals that parents should avoid?*

A: The worst chemical is a carcinogen called 1, 4 dioxane. It is found in a lot of kids' bath products, including bubble bath, as well as skin lotion. Other chemicals to avoid are phtalates and parabens. Many of these chemicals are made from petrochemicals so they contribute to global warming. They also accumulate in the environment and in our bodies.

Q: *How can parents teach their kids to learn which products are safe and which aren't?*

A: Parents can tell older kids that these bad products are made from oil and that this is what is causing America to be dependent upon foreign oil. For younger children, parents can simply explain that healthier products are better for them and better for penguins and polar bears (or any of their favorite animals.)

Greensourcing

Hair and Nail Salons: A day out at the beauty salon should leave you feeling clean and beautiful, not laden with toxic chemicals. Find out which products your local salon uses and ask if they will use organic hair and skin care products upon request. Aveda (**www.aveda.com**) products are made from organic, plant-based and non-petroleum ingredients. The company offsets all of their manufacturing practices with wind energy programs and continually campaigns to raise money for environmental and social causes. Their spas and hair salons can be found nationwide. If you live in New York City, check out the organic nail salon Priti (**www.pritiorganicspa.com**), founded by a mom-to-be who became frustrated by her doctor's recommendation to avoid nail salons during her pregnancy. Priti offers manicures, pedicures, waxing, facials, and massage using only 100% organic products and non-toxic paints.

Get The Kids Involved

- **Eco-Detectives:** It won't take long before your child develops strong preferences when it comes to personal care products. Teach her how to read labels and look for ingredients that are dangerous to her health so that she will be able to make better decisions about which products she wants to slather on her face.

- **Homemade Bubble Bath:** This bubble bath is so easy to make and use that you will wonder why you ever bought a commercial product. Little kids can help you measure out and combine the ingredients while older children can handle the whole project on their own. Combine 1 cup baby shampoo or eco-friendly liquid soap with ¾ water, and ½ to 1 teaspoon glycerin in a reusable plastic bottle. Add a few drops to running water at bath time for a fun, bubbly, nourishing bath. As an added perk, add a few drops of essential oil such as lavender, orange, or chamomile directly to the bath water.

• **Green (and Blue and Red) Face Paint:** Face paint is always popular with younger kids. Make your own eco-friendly paints by blending ½ teaspoon diaper cream with 1 heaping teaspoon of cornstarch. Add a little water to get the paint to the desired consistency. Scoop the mixture into a few separate containers (such as egg cups or bottle caps) and add 1 or 2 drops of the food coloring of your choice to each. (These face paints will wash off with warm water, but be sure to take the usual precautions for allergies and clothes stains.)

Check The Labels

Look for these labels as you search for environmentally friendly beauty products. See **Green Shopping Tips** in Chapter 12 for the definitions.

U$e Your Green

Cosmetics: Aveda (www.aveda.com), Burt's Bees (www.burtsbees.com), and Perfect Organics (www.perfectorganics.com) offer rich and beautiful cosmetic selections that use organic and natural ingredients.

Personal Care Products: Check out the following sites for organic personal care products: Aveda (www.aveda.com), Burt's Bees (www.burtsbees.com), Desert Essence (www.desertessence.com), Dr. Hauschka (www.drhauschka.com), and Toms of Maine (www.tomsofmaine.com). Also, look for Recycline toothbrushes (www.recycline.com) made from 100% recycled plastic.

Resources

Compact For Safe Cosmetics
Safe Cosmetics
www.safecosmetics.org
Download a list of companies that have pledged to keep personal care products "cruelty-free."

EcoLabels
www.eco-labels.org
Detailed information about the labels on your favorite personal care products

Skin Deep
Environmental Working Group
www.cosmeticsdatabase.com
A comprehensive campaign to inform consumers about the toxins in personal care products

Chapter 17:

Green Gifts and Parties

Let's face it, holidays and birthdays just wouldn't be the same without the giving and receiving of gifts. But that doesn't mean you need to go over-board or buy gifts that go against your conscience. The best gift is one that is perfect for the recipient and gentle on the environment. Here's how to find green gifts for everyone on your list.

Top 5 Ways To Make An Impact

1. **Give Consumables:** Everybody needs to eat, right? Consumable gifts such as cookies, organic teas, or fresh flowers make a thoughtful gift for almost any occasion and produce very little waste. And besides, who doesn't love a batch of gooey, fresh baked cookies or a crispy loaf of fresh baked bread?

2. **Offer Up Your Services:** Skip the material gift and offer your services instead. Offer to baby sit, shovel snow, make dinner, develop a website, weed the garden, wash the dog, or run an errand (the possibilities are endless).

3. **Offer Up Someone Else's Services:** No time to do it yourself? Give a gift certificate for a service such as a massage or a green housecleaner.

4. **Support A Cause:** What do you buy for the friend who has everything? Consider donating to a charity that is near and dear to the recipient's heart. See **Use Your Green** for charitable gift ideas for everyone on your shopping list.

5. **The Wrap Up:** Regular wrapping paper costs a bundle and lasts but a few minutes before it hits the trash bin. Consider a green alternative such as a reusable bag or basket, a scarf, or recycled materials such as newspaper or brown paper bags. You can make your package beautiful with natural adornments such as flowers or pine cones. If you need to mail the package, replace plastic bubble wrap and Styrofoam peanuts with eco alternatives such as crumpled newspaper, pine needles, or straw.

Green Tips

Turn Up The Green

Keep the environment in mind when you purchase gifts by looking for fair-trade, organic, or locally grown options whenever possible. If it's appropriate, consider giving a gift such as a low-flow showerhead or a basketful of compact fluorescent light bulbs to get a friend started on the eco path (this makes a great wedding or housewarming gift).

Make It Yourself

If you have the skills, consider making a handmade gift that is much more likely to be cherished (and retained) by the receiver. Knit a baby blanket, put together a scrapbook, make a photo frame, or sew an apron for an easy low-impact gift.

Buy Local

Look for gifts that are produced close to home. Whether it's a basket of fresh vegetables from a local farm or a ceramic bowl made by a local potter, locally produced gifts reduce the emission and packaging involved in shipping.

Buy Preloved

Hit your local thrift shop, flea market, or vintage boutique to find a wide range of unique and time-tested gifts. If necessary, refurbish the item with a new coat of paint or a well placed ribbon to turn it into a gift the receiver will treasure.

No-Waste Gifts

Gift cards to a favorite restaurant or store are easy to give and popular to receive. Other no-waste gift ideas include tickets (movies, theater, or sporting events), club memberships, or charitable donations.

Unplug

Try to avoid giving gifts that will continue to produce waste or require electricity. If you have to give a power-hungry gift, throw in a package of rechargeable batteries and a charger to eliminate waste.

Give Green Toys

Look for FSC-certified wood and organic fabrics when choosing green toys for kids. And when you have to go with plastic, steer clear of soft plastic toys that are likely to contain polyvinyl chloride (PVC). The European Union recently banned the sale of toys containing PVC after studies found that these toys leached phthalates that may disrupt the natural development of hormones.

GREEN YOUR HOLIDAYS

Every year, Americans send out 7 billion greeting cards, use more than 38,000 miles of ribbon and throw away over $300 million in wrapping paper during holiday celebrations. Of course, no one wants to be Scrooge, or be forced to give up their favorite family traditions, in order to go green. But there are plenty of ways to celebrate with style without wreaking havoc on the planet. Here's how to celebrate your favorite holidays with green spirit.

Christmas/ Hanukkah/Kwanzaa

- Decorate with low-energy light bulbs that last longer than traditional bulbs but use 80 to 90% less energy. Invest in timers that automatically shut off your lights before you go to bed.

- Skip the paper cards and send e-cards or set up an online holiday slide show or photo album at sites such as Photobucket (**www.photobucket.com**) or Flickr (**www.flickr.com**).

- Get creative with gift wrapping. Use old maps, the Sunday comics, or your children's artwork to wrap gifts or use gift bags and decorative boxes that can be reused from year to year.

- Compost your Christmas tree or Kwanzaa mazao and vibunzi

- Save bows, ribbons, holiday cards, and other decorations to reuse next year.

- Purchase a reusable menorah or kinara and use soy-based candles to light your way.

- Prevent waste by realistically anticipating the amount of food your family can eat and compost any leftover food scraps.

Easter

- Buy eggs at your local farmer's market, or purchase organic eggs from the store.

- Shred scratch paper or old magazines to use as "grass" in your basket in place of the plastic variety. After the holiday, reuse the grass again for packing material or compost.

- DIY your DYE by using natural foods such as onion skins (yellow or red), beets, spinach, blueberries, coffee, tea, turmeric, or paprika to dye your eggs.

Halloween

- Raid the thrift store or your child's dress up box for costumes or host a costume exchange party to trade costume with friends.

- Hand out healthy treats to your trick-or-treaters, such as fair trade chocolates, organic raisins, individually-sealed bags of microwavable popcorn, and all-natural snack bars; or give out non-food items such as stickers, soy crayons, or temporary tattoos.

- Give your kids a reusable tote bag or sac to collect their Halloween treats

Valentine's Day

- Save the paper and send your loved one a mushy e-card

- Show your love (for your beau and the planet) with organic flowers or chocolates.

Interview with Green Parent Corey Colwell-Lipson

As a wise frog once said, "It ain't easy being green." That's especially true around the holidays, when even the greenest parents tend to go a little crazy. Because let's face it, no parent wants her kids to miss out on all of the fun and traditions that holidays have to offer. But one mom, Green Parent Corey Colwell-Lipson, got tired of selling her soul in an effort to celebrate holidays with her two children, aged 6¾ and 3. So she decided to challenge the way we look at holidays. Her first target: Halloween. Through her organization, Green Halloween (**www.greenhalloween.org**), Corey found ways to involve the whole family in keeping the great parts about the holiday while losing the wasteful, unhealthy stuff. Here's what Green Parent Corey Colwell-Lipson had to say about candy, costumes, and turning tradition on its ear.

Q: Why did you decide to start Green Halloween?

A: Last year, when I took my kids trick-or-treating, I noticed that a few of the houses gave away non-candy items like stickers or bubbles. I was so excited to see this, and even more excited that my kids, and all of the other kids we ran in to, were so excited about it. It suddenly occurred to me that Halloween didn't have to be about candy; that it could be healthier. And that got me thinking that if it could be healthier, why couldn't it be more earth-friendly? It seemed to me that the time was right to introduce this to people.

I started sharing my idea with people and every single person that I spoke with, both young and old, thought it was a great idea. Initially I was focused on trick-or-treating but it gradually expanded out to the whole holiday, because trick-or-treating isn't the only unhealthy, un-earth-friendly tradition that's involved in Halloween. There are lots of ways that we can overhaul the holiday and still keep it fun and family-oriented to create the good memories but lose some of the things that a lot of us were feeling guilty about.

Q: *What advice do you have for parents who want to have a more eco-friendly holiday, but don't want to give up all of the fun?*

A: When it comes to human nature, you need to focus on the glass being half full. If you just make it sound like you are trying to take away the goodies, then kids will probably say "no, thanks." But if you don't discuss what you're not getting, and instead you discuss what you are going to do, then my experience is that everyone will be on board.

Parents need to look at what the alternatives are, and how they can keep them fun while maintaining your family's traditions. It's not about depriva-tion; it's about doing something good, feeling really good about it and keeping all of the great things about your holidays. Science backs the fact that people feel good when they do good things for other people and for the planet.

Q: *What are your thoughts about the other holidays?*

A: It's always been written in to Green Halloween's mission to eventually address all of the holidays. There can be healthy and earth-friendly alter-natives woven in to any holiday, just like with our daily lives. It's really no different. But certainly, there are some holidays that cry out for a little bit more overhaul than others. Halloween was an obvious place to start, but other holidays like Easter, Valentine's Day, and the winter holidays, where there is a lot of excess of unhealthy and un-earth-friendly traditions, those are the one's we're going to address next.

Q: *How do you get your kids involved in the Green Halloween spirit?*

A: I think that getting your kids involved is really the best place to start. What is so fascinating to me is that it seems to be the adults who are stuck doing things the way they have always done it; whereas the kids are open to trying something new. Most children nowadays have some information about the fact that our planet is not in the best state right now and that it's their responsibility to find ways to take care of it. It seems that school-aged kids are so excited about finding ways to help the planet and to help other people. So they just need to be given the opportunity and the chance to be heard and let their creativity go from there.

My suggestion for parents is to have a conversation with your kids and let them know that you're looking for ways to make your family holidays better for the environment and for other people. Ask them: "What are your ideas about that?" Teenagers seem to really get in to the details about what's going on with the planet and feel empowered when they realize that they can do things about it. For young ones, like my three-year-old, we just make the decision and set the example as a parent. Because for kids this age, it's our job as parents to make the decision on issues of nutrition and consumerism. Children aren't going to do the research as to the long and short term implications of various chemicals and things that are in candy. That's the parent's job.

How To Throw A Great Green Party

Whether it's a baby's birthday bash or an adult-only soiree, keep your next gathering green with these easy tips:

Invites: Save money and resources by sending invites via email or text message. If you need to send an invitation by snail mail, make sure it is printed on recycled paper.

Decorations: Skip the paper and plastic and decorate with natural items from your backyard such as plants, flowers, and pinecones. Pick up reusable decorations such as pillows, scarves, and other fabrics. If your child just loves balloons, don't deprive him, but make those balloons work hard to earn their place at the party. Use them as decorations and as parting gifts for friends (just make sure at least one stays home for the guest of honor).

Party Supplies: If possible, use reusable dishes, utensils, and cloth napkins. If you do need to use paper products, seek out those with the highest recycled paper content or compostable utensils. Rent or borrow items that you won't need more than once, like large punch bowls, chaffing dishes, or insulated beverage containers.

Gift Bags: Replace the bags of gift junk with eco-friendly gifts such as consumables (cookies or lollipops are always a hit for kids, or try plants or flowers for adults), tickets (sporting events, movies, museums), or reusables (picture frames or art supplies).

Food: Avoid waste by thinking conservatively when planning the quantity of food to serve guests. You will save a bundle of time and money in food preparation and cleanup. Be sure to donate any extra non-perishable items to your local food shelter.

Trash: Set up recycling areas near your trash cans so that guests can easily recycle cans, paper, and glass.

U$e Your Green

Need a green gift idea for your child, your parents, or anyone in between? Here are a few gift ideas for everyone on your shopping list:

Moms

The Flower Lover: If the lady in your life loves flowers, consider sending her an organic flower bouquet. Check out the selections from Organic Bouquet (**www.organicbouquet.com**) or California Organic Flowers (**www.californiaorganicflowers.com**).

The Chocoholic: There are a number of decadent organic chocolate selections that are sure to please chocolate lovers. Here's a few good one's to try: Dagoba Organic Chocolate (**www.dagobachocolate.com**), Green & Black's (**www.greenandblacks.com**), and Newman's Own Organic Chocolate (**www.newmansownorganics.com**).

Pamper Her: Help your mom renew her energy with a pampering gift from Aveda (**www.aveda.com**), Dr. Hauschka (**www.drhauschka.com**), or Desert Essence (**www.desertessence.com**).

A Gift That Gives Back: Check out The Charity Navigator (**www.charitynavigator.org**) to find a charitable organization to match the interests of any mom on your list. The independent site lists charities by category and gives detailed information about the mission, efficiency, and capacity of thousands of organizations.

Dads

The Sports Nut: If your dad likes to go green on the green, why not give him a set of water-soluble golf balls from Eco Golf Balls (**www.ecogolfballs.com**) or biodegradable golf tees from Eco Golf (**www.ecogolf.com**)?

Eco Gadgets: Boys can't resist their toys, so gadgets such as a hand-crank flashlight for the car or a solar-powered radio for the boat are sure to be a hit. Check out Sundance Solar (**http://store.sundancesolar.com**) for a number of eco-gadget selections.

Offset Him: Offset dad's carbon footprint with a gift of renewable energy credits (RECs) or greentags. The money you spend on carbon offsets will be used to support a renewable energy project, thereby "offsetting" dad's carbon emissions. Check out Carbon Neutral (**www.carbonneutral.com**) or Green Tags USA (**www.greentagsusa.org**) to calculate carbon emissions and purchase greentags.

Kids

Newborns: Look for organic stuffed toys from sites such as Gaiam (**www.gaiam.com**), or consider a teddy bear from Eco-Artware (**www.eco-artware.com**) that is made from clean, recycled fabric.

Seuss-Magic and other Great Books: The Lorax, by Dr. Seuss, is the absolute standard when it comes to teaching kids about environmental awareness. Other great books include *The Magic Schoolbus: At The WaterWorks* by Joanna Cole, Carl Haissen's Hoot about the destruction of the Everglades, and the Gaia Girl series by Lee Welles (think eco-savvy Nancy Drew).

For Eco-Engineers: Mechanically inclined kids will love an eco-toy that helps them learn a little about the environment while building something fun. DIY solar power kits or hydrogen model cars are usually easy to find at your local hobby shop. Gaiam (www.gaiam.com) makes a Power House Kit that gives kids the supplies they need to build a model house complete with PV solar panels, wind turbine, greenhouse, and desalination system. The kit comes with an illustrated manual that includes 70 experiments and 20 building activities.

The Little Idealist: Even the youngest recipient will be delighted with a charitable gift that piques her interest. Does the kid on your list love books? Donate her favorite title to the local library. Does he love the outdoors? Give him a gift membership to the Sierra Club (www.sierraclub.org) or the Nature Conservancy (www.nature.org). For more ideas check out Idealist.org (www.idealist.org) for a listing of charitable groups that were founded by kids.

Eco-Friendly Sweets: If your child has a sweet tooth (and what child doesn't!) he will love making his own treats with a Glee Kit (www.gleegum.com). Choose between the Chewing Gum Kit, the Gummy Candy Kit, and the Chocolate Kit. Each one comes with all of the ingredients necessary to make the treat as well as fun stories and information about the origins of the candy.

Everyone Else

Grandparents: Keep it simple by giving grandparents gifts they will treasure. Pictures of the grandkids, handmade artwork, or a DVD of home movies will please Grandma time and time again.

Babysitters: A good babysitter is a person to treasure. Pamper yours with a gift card to her favorite shop or restaurant.

Budding Environmentalists: Need a gift for a friend that has a blossoming interest in environmental issues? Try putting together a little starter kit of eco-goodies such as a CFL light bulb, green cleaning agents, a low-flow showerhead, and some scrumptious organic goodies. Pack it all in a reusable shopping tote and your friend will be ready to save the planet!

The Eco-Clueless: Friends who don't even register environmental issues on their radar will still love a gift from Ten Thousand Villages (www.tenthousandvillages.com), a one-stop shop for fair-trade items brought to you from literally hundreds of local artisans groups in Asia, Africa, Latin America, and the Middle East. They carry everything from silk scarves to jewelry to recycled tote bags in a wide range of prices and styles. Be sure to enclose the artisan information with your gift so your recipient can see the face behind the item.

The New Parents: Any new (or current!) parents need a copy of *The Green Parent: A Kid-Friendly Guide to Earth-Friendly Living*. You can even tell them how much you love your copy!

Get The Kids Involved

- **Handmade Gifts:** Encourage your kids to give hand-made gifts to their friends and family that minimize waste while showing how much they care. Even the youngest children can help color a picture or glue together a picture frame for a loved one. Older kids can choose a project that matches their skills.

- **Wrapping It Up:** Skip the fancy wrapping paper and wrap your presents in paper that your children design. Use plain recycled scrap paper or reuse a brown paper bag to cover the present and let your kids jazz it up with markers, crayons, paints, and stamps.

- **Art Cards:** Scan your child's latest artwork into your computer and use it to create your own unique recycled paper cards. Check out Conservatree (www.conservatree.org) for a listing a retailers that sell blank eco-friendly note cards. (Print out a stack of these cards and tie with a ribbon for a great gift for the grandparents!)

Resources

Care 2 Greenliving
  25 Great Consumer-Less Gift Ideas
  http://www.care2.com/greenliving/25-great-consumer-less-gift-ideas.html

Grist, Environmental News and Commentary
  www.grist.org

Sierra Club
  Green Gift Ideas
  http://www.sierraclub.org/e-files/gift_ideas.asp

The Natural Resource Defense Council
  Great Green Gift-Giving Guide
  http://www.nrdc.org/cities/living/ggift.asp

Treehugger
  www.treehugger.com
  Green Yourself

Chapter 18:

All About You

O.K., now that you have taken care of the kids, the house, your work, your child's school, the groceries, the cleaning, and everything else, it is finally time for you. If you have any time, energy, and motivation left, use these ideas to become the Green Parent you always thought you would be (before you had kids!).

Top 5 Ways To Make An Impact

1. **Learn:** Get informed about environmental issues so that you can make the best eco-friendly decisions for yourself and your family. Surf the web, pick up a good book, or watch a movie (see below for suggestions) to arm yourself with knowledge and ideas.

2. **Vote:** Use the power of the ballot to send a clear message to elected officials about your environmental concerns. Browse the environmental record of potential candidates at the League of Conservation Voters (www.lcv.org) and be sure to let them know what you think. Check out

The Green Parent (www.thegreenparent.com) to download letters you can send to Congress asking them to make the environment a priority.

3. **Get Involved:** Get involved in the environmental issues that affect your community. Organize a recycling center or used clothing drop-off location. Encourage your local utility company to offer discounts or rebates on energy- and water-saving products. Lead a trash clean-up day. Or, write an editorial letter to your local paper about the environment initiatives that could give your community a boost.

4. **Join The Club:** Become a member of your favorite environmental organization, such as the Sierra Club (www.sierraclub.org), The Natural Resource Defense Council (www.nrdc.org), and the Humane Society (www.hsus.org) to support their efforts and stay informed about their latest campaigns.

5. **Give Back:** Give a little back to the environment by donating time or money to a charity that helps to protect the environment. Sponsor a local environmental club or organization, or check out the Charity Navigator (www.charitynavigator.org) or Idealist (www.idealist.org) to find an environmentally friendly campaign that interests you.

Interview with Green Parent Bill McKibben

Bill McKibben is a respected environmentalist and author of a number of environmental books including *The End of Nature, The Age of Missing Information, Hope, Human, and Wild, Fight Global Warming Now,* and *Deep Economy*. In 2006, Bill led a five-day walk across Vermont to demand action on global warming (it was considered by many to be the largest climate change demonstration to date in America). In 2007, he founded Step It Up 2007 (**www.stepitup2007.org**) and organized 1,400 global warming demonstrations across all 50 states to demand that Congress take action on climate change. Bill is also the proud Green Parent of a teenaged daughter. Here's what Bill McKibben had to say about the environment, bicycles, and fast food.

Q: *Parents are often led to believe that they can buy their way to a happier family by investing in items that will theoretically save them time and money. These are often the items (fast foods, disposable diapers, chemical cleaning agents) that get us in to the most trouble with the environment. What advice do you have for parents who see the needs of the environment as conflicting with those of their family?*

A: My guess is that in most cases environmental goals and family goals are closely correlated. For instance, fast food is pretty much an environmental mess—cheap food grown under dubious conditions and trucked long distances that makes kids fat. But it's also a social mess—eaten fast, in noisy and anonymous buildings. A simple dinner prepared fast but with some love and care and shared together, even for a few minutes, around the table brings a family into focus. It's hard to imagine my own family in its absence.

Q: *Where do you think parents should focus their environmental efforts in order to have the most beneficial impact (greener cars, shorter showers, recycling)?*

A: Anything that truly addresses energy use, which is our particular problem. So, put in insulation, lots of it. Buy a hybrid car or better yet buy a bike (it's nice that our most traditionally kid-friendly means of transport is also the most eco-friendly).

Q: *Do you have any advice for parents who want to find a way to promote environmental stewardship that does not sound like "eco-nagging" in the ears of their children?*

A: Get them politically involved in the environmental movement, so they can see that it really means something. When we did our 1,400 Step It Up demonstrations last spring to stop global warming, almost every picture showed lots and lots of kids involved.

Curl Up With A Great Green Read

Sand County Almanac, by Aldo Leopold

Silent Spring, by Rachel Carson

The End of Nature, by Bill McKibben

The Ecology of Commerce, by Paul Hawken

Desert Solitaire, by Edward Abbey

Deep Economy, by Bill McKibben

Down To Earth: Nature's Role In American History, by Ted Steinberg

Worldchanging: A User's Guide To The 21st Century, by Alex Steffen

Cadillac Desert: The American West and Its Disappearing Water, by Marc Reisner

An Inconvenient Truth: The Crisis of Global Warming, by Al Gore

Catch A Green Flick

Planet Earth, The Complete BBC Series

An Inconvenient Truth

Who Killed The Electric Car

Surf The Green

Green Parenting

www.grizzlybird.net/greenparenting.html
Green parenting thoughts and tips from GreenDaddy and MaGreen

Grist, Environmental News and Commentary
www.grist.org

Ideal Bite
www.idealbite.com

The Green Guide
www.thegreenguide.com
National Geographic's guide to green living

The Green Parent
www.thegreenparent.com

The League of Conservation Voters
(202) 785-8683
www.lcv.org
See how your elected officials rate on their "National Environmental Scorecard."

Treehugger
www.treehugger.com

Worldchanging
www.worldchanging.com

Chapter 19:
Going Further

Ready to do even more? For the bold, the brave and the *uber*-motivated, check out these resources to help you reach an even deeper shade of green:

Hypermiling

Hypermiling, or driving for the maximum fuel efficiency, goes beyond the standard fuel efficiency tips of inflating tires and parking in the shade. Hypermilers regularly practice techniques such as drafting behind 18-wheelers and hitting interstate exit ramps without hitting the brakes. On the opposite end of the spectrum, hypermilers also accelerate at a crawl and avoid jackrabbit driving, all in an effort to save gas. Does it work? Dedicated hypermilers often get at least 50% more miles per gallon than the rest of us. Check out Hypermiling (**www.hypermiling.com**) to learn more.

Unplugging

In a growing number of homes around the nation, Americans are doing more than conserving energy, they are making their own. Roughly 180,000 homes currently supply all of their own power using renewable sources such as solar, wind, hydro, or geothermal. Ready to go off-the-grid? Check out Off-Grid (http://off-grid.net) to get started.

The Compact

The Compact began as a New-Year's challenge among friends, when a small group of San Francisco acquaintances pledged not to buy any new products for one year. The members made a few exceptions, such as food, medication, and underwear, but generally agreed to avoid all consumption in an effort to simplify their lives and reduce their environmental impact. Like all great and interesting ideas, the story of the Compact flew across the world, inspiring sister groups, documentaries, and a flurry of web information. Check out the original blog that started it all at http://sfcompact.blogspot.com.

Interview with Green Parent Colin Beaven

Do you ever wonder if it is possible to live on this planet and raise a family without contributing to the environmental mess? Green Parent Colin Beaven did. So in November of 2006, he embarked upon a year-long experiment with his wife (Michelle), his two-year old daughter (Isabella), and his dog (Frankie) that he dubbed "No Impact Man," in a philosophical attempt to completely wipe out his ecological footprint. The plan was to slowly phase out all methods of ecological destruction and work towards environmental improvement. I chatted with Colin (and Isabella) about ten months into their experiment.

Q: *You decided to phase in the "No Impact" experiment over a period of one year. Can you tell me a bit more about the different phases of your experiment?*

A: No trash, no carbon-producing transportation, sustainable eating, sustainable consumption, no electricity, water conservation, and finally, giving back. We're at the giving back stage now which basically means I'm doing volunteer work.

Q: *Do you feel like you have achieved your "No Impact" goals?*

A: It's not intended to be scientific; it's intended to be philosophical. There is no way to truly be no impact. Even if you do positive things you are still causing a negative impact in another area. But the question is, "Is it possible to do more good than harm living on this planet?" So, do I think I've done more good than harm? I'd like to think so.

Q: *Will you continue to live the "No Impact" lifestyle past the one-year mark? Is this your new way of life?*

A: Well, for the purposes of this one year, things are pretty extreme. We don't use the elevator. We don't use the laundry machine. So I think we'll be looking at more of a middle ground afterwards. But what's interesting is that if we had started from where we were at a year ago (because we were just like everybody else) and tried to cut down, we would not be doing nearly as much as we are now where we have cut away everything and now we're going to add a few things back.

Q: *What has been the hardest phase for you?*

A: Everybody asks what has been the hardest for me and I think that's really interesting, because that's an assumption that it would be hard, or that the project would be a matter of deprivation. But actually, we've found that there are lots of benefits to the project. There are a bunch of psychologists that point out that if we think that consumption and buying more stuff is going to make us happy we're mistaken. The things that actually make us happy are things like putting more emphasis on our relationships, living according our values, connecting to something larger and putting more meaning into our lives. And the project has allowed for a lot of that. Like getting rid of the TV. We didn't know this was going to happen, but it caused the family to come together more because we entertain each other instead of passively watching TV. We eat together and cook together and wash the dishes together instead of eating out of a bunch of plastic takeout cups. So when people ask me what I'm going to give up about the project when it's over, I think, what should I give up? The fact that I'm eating more healthily or that I spend more time with my daughter?

But that's the long answer to your question. The short answer is ... the hardest thing is not having a laundry machine!

Q: *Was this project especially challenging for you to do with a child?*

A: No, it's actually the opposite. Isabella is the leader of the project. I once heard about a Zen master who was asked by a parent, "When do we start teaching our children Zen?" The teacher laughed and said, "We don't teach them Zen, they teach us Zen."

Early on in the project, when I was still getting used to the idea of not rushing around by subway or car, I took Isabella out and we were going to go to the park. On our way she stopped at a fire hydrant. There was a little chain that hung off it and she poked it with her finger and watched it swing back and forth. She poked it again and I said, "Come on Isabella, let's go the park and have fun." And then we walked a little bit further and she started playing with this pole and I said, "Come on, we gotta go have fun." I finally realized that we were already having fun. That was really germane to the project because we have this idea that you have to buy stuff or watch TV to have fun. And this has all taught me that maybe I need to look for the fun in the moment rather than being told where to look for fun.

Q: *Which phase of the project was the most successful for you and your family?*

A: The "no carbon-producing transportation" means that we've been on our bicycles, which is no end of joy for us. We got this new rickshaw today. (I say new, but it's made from entirely secondhand parts.) We ride around on our bikes all of the time now and we really love it so that's been successful. The local eating means that we don't do the takeout thing and we actually eat together around the table. So, that has been really successful. The fact that we don't have a TV is really good for our family. And just the general fact that we feel we're making an effort is really good for us because it makes us feel like we're not contributing to the problem as much as we were.

Q: *Do you have any advice for parents that are hoping to reduce their own impact?*

A: This whole thing is not rocket science, and it's not new. My grandparents told me not to waste. So just look at your life and ask yourself, where am

I wasting resources? For instance, why leave your house heated when no one is in it? Could you get a smart thermostat or something like that? Look for the waste. It will be different for each of us. I don't use non carbon-producing transportation, but if you live in the suburbs, you have no choice. But on the other hand, I can't turn my heat down because I live in an apartment whereas someone who lives in the suburbs can control their heat.

Now some people may find it too daunting to change the way they live. They could get involved in the political process. I'm not saying they should be liberal or conservative, because I don't consider this a partisan issue. But we can all convince both our liberal conservative representatives that we care about the planet and would like to do something about it.

The 100-Mile Diet

Based on the premise that the ingredients in the average North American meal travel at least 1,500 miles to get to the dinner table, Canadians Alisa Smith and James MacKinnon decided to try a little experiment. For one year, they would only eat foods that came from within 100 miles of their apartment in Vancouver, British Columbia. The couple launched into the experiment the hard way (with no prior planning) and wound up losing a lot of weight and eating a lot of potatoes. But their idea caught on, and now they offer resources to people around the world who want to try it. According to their website (http://100milediet.org), "A more realistic approach is to plan a single, totally 100-mile meal with friends or family, and see where you want to go from there."

The Great Green Beyond

It's hard to get excited about death. But like it or not, it is one of those facts of life that we all inevitably have to deal with. Green burials, which involve no embalming, no grave lining and biodegradable caskets, are growing in popularity. Want to learn more? Check out the Green Burial Council (**www.greenburialcouncil.org**) to learn how to make your departing an eco-friendly one.

Sources

Chapter 2: Water, Water, Everywhere

[1] Olson, Erik, "Bottled Water: Pure Drink or Pure Hype?" Natural Resources Defense Council, February 1999.

Chapter 3: Talkin' Trash

[2] Retrieved from http://www.nrc-recycle.org/top10itemstorecycle.aspx on August 6, 2007

Chapter 4: Green Clean

[3] "Safe Alternatives To Household Hazardous Products" Retrieved from http://www.sierraclub.ca/national/programs/health-environment/pesticides/alternative-household-prod.pdf on August 6, 2007

Chapter 5: How Green Is Your Yard?

[4] Retrieved from http://www.fws.gov/contaminants/Documents/Homeowners_Guide_Frogs.pdf on August 6, 2007

[5] Nishioka, M. et al, " Distribution of 2,4-D in air and on surfaces inside residences after lawn applications: comparing exposure estimates from various media for young children" *Environmental Health Perspectives*, Nov. 2001.

[6] Retrieved from http://www.epa.gov/ttn/atw/hlthef/di-oxyac.html on August 6, 2007

Chapter 7: Adding On?

[7] Retrieved from http://www.epa.gov/iaq/voc.html, on August 6, 2007

Chapter 8: Green Your Ride

[8] Retrieved from www.fueleconomy.gov on July 31, 2007.

Chapter 9: The Little Green Schoolhouse

[9] Wargo, J. *Children's Exposure To Diesel Exhaust on Schoolbuses* Environment and Human Health, Inc. Feb. 2002.

[10] Allaway, D. "Food choices in schools: Taste great, less waste!" Resource Recycling, Feb. 1995.

Chapter 10: Working Green
    [11] Retrieved from http://www.grist.org/biz/tp/2006/03/02/makower/ on August 6, 2007

Chapter 12: Green Shopping Tips
    [12] Food Marketing Institute, *US Grocery Shopper Trends*, 2002.

Chapter 13 Food: Eating Your Greens
    [13] Retrieved from http://www.downtoearth.org/articles/organic_facts.htm on August 8, 2007

    [14] Blondell J. Epidemiology of pesticide poisonings in the United States, with special reference to occupational cases. J Occup Med. 1997; 12:209-220.

    [15] Clay, J. "World agriculture and Environment," Island Press, 2004.

    [16] Retrieved from http://www.fda.gov/Fdac/features/895_brstfeed.html on August 8, 2007

    [17] Retrieved from http://www.foodnews.org/ on August 8, 2007

Chapter 16: Green Beauty
    [18] Retrieved from http://www.cir-safety.org/staff_files/publist.pdf on August 8, 2007

    [19] Environmental Working Group (2003). Body Burden. Pollution in People. January 2003. Retrieved from http://www.ewg.org/reports/bodyburden/index.php on August 8, 2007

    [20] Retrieved from http://www.grist.org/advice/ask/2005/06/06/umbra-shaving/index.html on August 5, 2007

Cut this card out and keep it in your wallet so you'll never be caught in the produce section without it!

Organic Top Ten

The Green Parent

1. Peaches
2. Apples
3. Baby Foods
4. Peanut Butter
5. Bell Peppers
6. Berries
7. Imported Grapes
8. Beef
9. Dairy Products
10. Eggs

Flip this page over and you'll find a handy list of "Chemicals to Avoid in Your Cosmetics".

Cut this card out and keep it in your wallet so you'll never be caught in the beauty section without it!

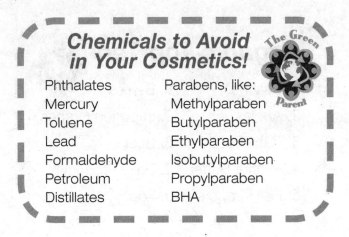

Chemicals to Avoid in Your Cosmetics!

The Green Parent

Phthalates
Mercury
Toluene
Lead
Formaldehyde
Petroleum
Distillates

Parabens, like:
Methylparaben
Butylparaben
Ethylparaben
Isobutylparaben
Propylparaben
BHA

Flip this page over and you'll find a handy list of "Organic Top Ten".

Index